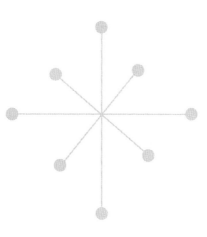

The Cliff Johnson Story

Up There with the Big Boys

as told to F. Dean Lueking

UP THERE WITH THE BIG BOYS

Designed and Printed by McLeod-Smith Graphics, Inc.
Oak Park, Illinois

Additional books are available by contacting: www.curf.edu/~crfjohnsoc

Printed in the United States of America

Table of Contents

Foreword

Cliff Johnson's life journey, which is still unfolding, is a fascinating kaleidoscope of unexpected turns.

His roots run deep in his South Dakota prairie beginnings in a farm family of sound Norwegian Lutheran piety. As Garrison Keillor's dead-on accurate radio portrayals from mythical Lake Woebegone, Norwegian Lutherans are modestly reticent folks who don't like to stand out in a crowd but—much like the second violins in the orchestra—are steady and stolid accompaniment in the background. Here is the story of a Norwegian Lutheran for whom standing out in a crowd of people comes as naturally as breathing. When at a tender age he stood on a cultivator seat and spoke to corn stalks, imagining their green shoots waving in the prairie wind as an applauding audience, something out of the ordinary was emerging. He was hooked on people, drawn to them in all their fascinating human variety. When puberty came and his voice changed, an awareness began to dawn on him that in his resonant voice he had an instrument that would mark his identity and be essential to his work throughout his lifetime.

Along with that early naturalness in talking with people came another fascination that gripped him as a fourth grader, never to let go. It was the arrival in the 1920's of the radio as a transforming new factor in American life.

To the triad of deep roots, deep voice, and deep people skills was added the radio as the medium that put him, and later his family, into the homes of thousands of American families every morning, first in the midwest and then coast-to-coast. These are among the elements that weave in and out of the Cliff Johnson story here told. But there is a deeper story line than runs beneath the swift career rise to become a household name in network radio, the celebrities interviewed, the countries and dignitaries visited, the zany events, and the unexpected turns of his career.

That underlying story is about a calling. That means something other than a professional career, something deeper than the constant pressure of self-invention. How does a young man, once headed for the pastoral vocation but then side-tracked by circumstances, discover his true and deeper calling as a Christian smack in the middle of the fast-track world of entertainment and journalism that offers more hostile landscape than encouraging paths? Cliff Johnson has carried a lifelong burden in not becoming the pastor that family expectations and his own early aspirations indicated. As his story here told suggests, his octogenarian accomplishment of finishing his academic degree, both at the baccalaureate and graduate levels, formed a kind of closure on that guilt baggage he has long carried. But the more important thing that broadens his story toward a wider relevance is how this talented man, well tested by all the ups and downs of life in front of a microphone reaching vast audiences, bumping elbows with the famous and those little known, discovered how essential is the grace of God is and how often that grace came to him in the partnership of his devoted spouse.

That's the other deep strand in the Cliff Johnson vocation, his wife and family. The Johnsons present a picture of a family, serious about avoiding the lethal dangers of celebrity status while unavoidably thrust into the public eye, and conscious of the challenge of putting values ahead of the toxic anxiety brought on by constant vying for top billing. That, too, is part of this deeper story, marriage and family as foundational to the

Christian calling, and how that has played out in decades when both marriage and family have taken a pounding.

Finally, a comment about the teller of this as-told-to narrative of Clifford Tilman Johnson. I am his pastor. That is both promising and perilous. The peril, of course, is that the story is little more than puffery or a whitewash with me as the uncritical booster of a parishioner with interesting credentials. That is what neither of us has sought and it will be up to the reader to decide how successful we have been as a team, Johnson the teller and Lueking the scribe. The promise of this combination, however, is that a pastor collaborating with a parishioner through a story, admittedly an unusual one, can place it the bigger story in which each of us has a part. That, I would hope, is a clue as to how all of us in the community of faith find ways to discover, lift up, and affirm the Good News at work in a world that needs it. I would never have come to know Cliff Johnson without the congregation that brought us together a half century ago. We thought we knew each other earlier. We've come to know each other much deeper through the more recent hours of talking together. We tell the story unfolding through these pages in the hope that it will inform and inspire, bring laughter and tears, perhaps, and when put aside offer food for thought on how remarkable, how wonderfully remarkable, it is to be alive and part of the ongoing human story.

F. Dean Lueking
March 24, 2004

CHAPTER 1

Cliffie, You're Special!

t was a day not unlike the smooth flow of many another routine day in a South Dakota farm household. Three generations of Johnsons shared the modest frame home and life was harmonious in the main because there was neither time nor space for discord in the days immediately following World War I. Everybody had to work hard. Getting along was not a luxury but a necessity.

But this day in 1920 was chosen by the grandmother in the family to do something unusual. Dorothea Olson Johnson swept up her five-year-old grandson in her arms and set him on the kitchen table, legs dangling and his feet shod in shiny new white shoes. The bright red sweater she put on him was one she had recently knit herself. It was an occasion for which she prepared well. "Clifford Tilman Johnson," she declared, "you are special. Remember that. You are very special. You're going to learn to sing and talk, so that everybody in church—everybody!—CAN HEAR YOU IN THE BACK ROW!"

It wasn't as though young Clifford Tilman was the favorite in the family. Grandma Dorothea's heart had more than enough affection for Doris, Russell, and Joseph, the other siblings in the close-knit family where hugs and affirming words were spread around generously. But this moment

1

with her third grandchild was the sign of her growing awareness of some-thing indeed unusual about him. He loved nothing more than to sing from memory the family songs he picked up quickly, tell aloud the fairy tales he made up from his lively imagination, and recite Bible passages he learned from the family devotions around the dinner table.

The kitchen table declaration was an anointing of sorts. More than eighty years later Cliff Johnson remembered it as an infusion of confidence-building energy needed to meet the constant, risk-filled challenges in the decades following and the successes they brought. It's essence, "Cliffie, you're special" also had to be reclaimed when later occasions in life brought him face-to-face with his share of perils and heartaches.

Grandparents the world over, to be sure, are given to warm hearted hyperbole when speaking of their offspring. But then there are those almost seer-like moments when a flattering phrase moves out beyond passing sentiment to become the harbinger of prophetic intuition, home-spun and therefore all the more genuine, about a child who would indeed be special in ways undreamed of at the time.

Little could Dorothea Olson Johnson have imagined the future those three words portended for the blond curly top on the receiving end of her pro-nouncement. Yet, this five year old Cliffie—the diminutive form of his baptismal name Clifford that has prevailed lifelong—has held that kitchen table moment in his memory with unfading clarity and drawn upon it often for inspiration and motivation. Much as children the world over respond to words of affirming love, so did Clifford Tilman Johnson get an early taste of the power of words and, in his case, a taste for the power of words that he would speak over the next eight decades via radio and tele-vision transmission throughout the nation and well beyond.

The unique contours of meaning that the anointing words "Cliffie, you're special!" would carve out were fully improbable against the back ground of the times in which they were spoken. In 1920 life expectancy was 54.4 years; at this writing Cliffie is amazingly well and agile at 88. The average American annual income was $1267; no Johnson farmer came anywhere close to that number but the boy on the kitchen table has done well beyond his father or grandfather's imagining. A new house cost $3395 then, Cliff has owned homes valued at many times that number. In 1920 a loaf of bread cost 7 cents, 20 cents for a pound of pork; and gas was 14 cents a gallon. Since then the boy dubbed to be special has known cost of living levels that would have made Grandma Dorothea gasp in disbelief. But these contrasts are in external matters. The odds created by the improbable circumstances of the 1920's do not fit the deeper core of Grandma Dorothea's intuition about her grandson, one rooted in the Christ-given faith and values that she prized for Cliffie and all her off-spring above all else.

Dorothea Olson Johnson brought impressive credentials for sensing the qualities that make for an extraordinary life. She had come with her family as a girl of ten from Norway in 1869, and made the last leg of the long journey in an oxen-drawn wagon to what was then known as the South Dakota Territory. There she grew up, experiencing deadly snowstorms that would leave neighbors frozen to death within a few feet of shelter in blizzard whiteouts. She told stories of wind-whipped prairie fires that could wipe out a year's crops in an afternoon. Once she had snatched a neighbor girl, Christi Flen, from a massive prairie fire and tended her horrible burn wounds for sixteen days before death brought merciful relief. At age nineteen she made Johan Edvard Olson wait a full year before accepting his proposal. As his bride, she helped build their sod house on the treeless South Dakota prairie. Year after year they broke new land for cultivation, with Dorothea's gathering and bundling weeds and dried cornstalks as their only fuel for household warmth and a cooking fire. Fifteen years of marriage passed before she had a washing machine. In that same period of time she did all her sewing by hand before acquiring a foot-treadle sewing machine made her needlework easier.

She did all manner of gardening and canning, and amidst all the myriad chores and privations, joys and satisfactions of frontier life bore twelve healthy children into the world. The third in line was Joseph Edward, Cliffie's father.

She summarized what sustained her through thick and thin, as a wife, mother, grandmother and finally as a widow in a two page testimony written years after, at her kitchen table, commending of young Cliffie to a special future. After exhorting all to follow the Ten Commandments— each one noted with pointed life applications and prayer that her children would live faithfully in their baptismal covenant—she expressed her readiness to come to the end of her days with a peaceful heart, summing up a lifetime of piety, hard work, and countless satisfactions thus: I feel God's help, whether I live or die, and it will take all of eternity to thank Him.

Two early boyhood events became important links in the unfolding story of just what "Cliffie, you're special" might mean. At Christmas, 1922, Joseph Edward Johnson scraped enough cash together from his crop-sharing work on 160 acres near the town of Beresford, South Dakota, to buy a four string ukulele for his children. It was an instant fascination for Cliff, who took to it well enough to reach a seven-chord level of performance and teenage community stardom at county fairs, school and family gatherings. The ukulele love affair has been long lasting; he still gets a lively if not somewhat incredulous response from his classroom students with his spirited rendition of *Five Foot Two, Eyes Of Blue* as a guest lecturer in his eighties!

The other development was even more propitious for his future. With second grade school chum, John Fundingsland, he learned how to build a radio crystal receiver from a do-it-yourself kit from his friend's father, a shoemaker in town. Cliff was mesmerized by what he thought was miraculous. By winding copper wire around a stick of wood, attaching a tiny chunk of crystal from the working kit, transformed sound waves were captured and a wavelength was secured which delivered real voices and actual music, flying through the air with interrupted jolts of static that made it into a small attached earphone.

The debut one evening of this mysterious, magical thing called a radio was a proper family event. Cliff's mother, Ada Matilda Johnson, made a large wash pan of popcorn complete with home-churned sweet cream butter. Family and farm hands emptied the pan, making way for the tiny earphone, connected to the crystal set, to sit nestled at the bottom of the empty popcorn pan, thus amplifying the radio sound waves with the astonishing message: "This is KDKA, Pittsburgh!" This was a first for everyone present. None had ever heard sounds flying through the air and become audible out of a home-made crystal set radio in a farm kitchen wash pan. The excitement accelerated. There it was, the static-driven familiar sounds of a ukulele, strumming the hit tune of the times "Five Foot Two, Eyes Of Blue, oh what those five feet can do, has anybody seen my girl? Turned up nose, turned down hose, flapper yes sir, one of those, has anybody seen my girl?…"

There was stunned silence in the household, Cliff recalls. Grandma Dorothea, true to her Norwegian Lutheran piety which frowned on dancing and card playing, broke the silence with a question whether it was Satan or the Holy Ghost sending songs all the way from Pittsburgh about blue-eyed girls with turned down hose. But eight-year-old Cliffie was hooked. Caught up in jaw-dropping amazement by what he had just witnessed, he turned to his mother and announced: "Mom, that's what I want to do …sing and talk on the radio!" Grandma Dorothea's affirming words were turning up a new prospect of what was to become a lifelong vocation. Cliff teamed up with another second grader, a boy from town, to create the radio set. Cliff was a country boy, not a "townie" and the distinction mattered to second graders, especially to Cliff who had been bothered by the nickname "Moley" hung on him by other kids who teased him about the three moles on is right cheek. His second grade teacher, Elva Hensing, dealt with the matter deftly. Knowing his sensitivity over the teasing, she put him in charge of the phonics and math cards used in class. It was a boost at the time, and the radio discovery lifted his esteem a few notches higher.

The timing of the crystal set project was fortuitous. Radio was at the cusp of a new era following its beginnings in 1906 with a Christmas Eve program from an experimental station in Brant Rock, Mass. World War I brought further developments of radio as a means of communicating messages. In 1916 radio industry pioneer David Sarnoff entered the picture with the earliest format of what later became the National Broadcasting Company. Most historians of the subject agree that the first commercial radio station in the nation was KDKA in Pittsburgh, which was only two-years-old when the Johnson family heard it for the first time via the crystal set that two second graders had set up.

Grandma Dorothea's prophetic intuition took on an additional link two years later when a neighboring farmer, John Ytterness, made an inquiring comment to Cliff's dad about the sanity of his second son. "Strange things going on in the cornfield with your son…" he began. "I saw your Clifford standing on the plow-cultivator seat, singing and talking to the corn rows. When their leaves flapped in the wind, your boy seemed to take it as applause, and bowed to them for an encore." John Edward Johnson answered with a knowing grin, recalling Grandma Dorothea's comment that was becoming household gospel. "Clifford is going to sing in church Sunday, and he's practicing out in the cornfield so that everybody can hear him, especially those in the last row!" And that's what he did on the Sunday following, with John Ytterness among those smiling in approval in the back row with the look of one who had heard it rehearsed a few days before in a patch of corn.

Cliff's boyhood years were brightened by his father's acquiring a pony,

Nellie, from a fabrics peddler with the un-Norwegian, un-Lutheran, un-Dakota name Abraham Abdullah. It was an early experience in diversity. As a family the Johnsons could deal with someone that exotic, making the trade for the pony with a work horse plus ten dollars thrown in for good will. Cliff was euphoric, riding the pony to and from Silver Lake School, a three mile ride that went better and faster by pony rather than barefoot. When winter came and sudden snow storms threatened, the senior Johnson rigged up a safety rope with knots strategically placed so that pony and rider could not be separated by an ice-coated rope with no grip left. The precautionary measure was well placed. Boy and pony were caught in a sudden snowstorm one early winter day, but reached a neighbor's cave for initial shelter and then made it safely to the German family's house. What stuck in his memory was not only the hospitable German household, but the fact that they kept beer as a year-around staple for all in the family. He turned down the beer, but relished the conversation that included talk of "the Johnson kid" who was good at singing and speaking.

Sheltering neighbors caught in blizzards was but one form of neighborliness on the Dakota plains in the 1920's. The pioneer spirit was more than the quest for new land, gold, and railroad tracks beginning to crisscross the lands once dominated by Indians and buffalo. Clusters of Norwegians, other Scandinavian immigrant families, Germans and Irish made up the cultural mix of the region. While each had their individual congregations and holiday gatherings, the women especially crossed the boundaries of language and custom to help each other with the perils of childbirth in sod house surroundings. Temporary though such bonds were, they helped build a slender thread of community in times and places where community was not a political abstraction but a necessity to hold life together when emergencies threatened life and limb.

Early teen life on the prairie could produce hair-raising moments, as Cliff learned as a lad of fourteen. His father lost six registered dairy cows, a staggering loss in Depression times. They had broken through a fence into a field of spring alfalfa and literally ate themselves to death on the gas-producing chemicals that the chemistry of fresh alfalfa delivered to the bovine large intestinal tract. It was a Sunday afternoon when Cliff and his older brother, Russell, discovered the six cows already bloated by the alfalfa-gorging, dead from suffocation. Their father was gone. It was the hired man's day off. There was nothing to do but run to the alfalfa field where four registered golden Guernsey prize milk cows were already frozen into the final panting stage, bloated from the deadly alfalfa they could not resist. Russell yelled for Cliff to run home and get two sharp butcher knives. He dashed back in time to hand one knife to Russell and with his own trembling hand to summon all the strength he had to drive the knife through the thick cowhide into the cow's left side, just six inches to the left of the hip bone. The knife finally broke through, and the resulting explosion showered Cliff with gas and undigested alfalfa. Having succeeded with emergency veterinary medicine on the first two cows, the brothers went on to save the next two as well with the same stab-and-twist surgery on the spot. They were shaking and sweat was running down the faces, but they managed a forced smile at what they had accomplished. When their father returned home and learned of what happened, they were heroes, pleased that their story had made the rounds in the congregation and the town.

Cliff's high school years were, like every other teenagers on the Dakota prairie, directly affected by the triple calamity of Depression, drought, and dust storms in the 1930's. Despite the crisis that began with the stock market crash of 1929, his first several years of high school were a flurry of productive activity. With his energetic imagination in overdrive, he threw himself into his studies, drama and debate club participation, winning singing contests at the state level with his baritone voice now maturing, making the football and basketball team (at five-feet-five he claimed he could get around bigger opponents simply by dribbling under their armpits), showing leadership in student organizations, and all the while helping his dad with early morning farm chores. He wasn't unaware of the subtle put-downs of the town kids about the country kids since such talk was hardly subtle. But he could always depend on the willing, sacrificial support of his parents. In sports and music competition that called for transportation to a neighboring towns or the more distant Sioux Falls, Joseph and Ada Johnson were there to do the driving, cheering, and return-trip rehashing of how things went.

But the pressure of school activities and helping at home began to take its toll in his junior year. His dad had established a dairy route in nearby Beresford and had even managed to buy a Dodge truck to replace the horse and buggy deliveries. Helping his father make the forty stops on the delivery run meant skipping school days with increasing frequency. The principal called him in for a talk about his grades that were slipping. Things came to a head one evening at the supper table when the conversation, initiated by Cliff, turned to the prospect of his dropping out a year so that things could even out. With parental consent, reluctant though it was, that decision was made.

That year of 1932-'33 was a tough one. As Cliffie made the morning rounds delivering milk to forty customers, he regularly saw his classmates heading off to school and the sight did not cheer him. Despite many farm youth who dropped out of school for similar reasons in the toughest Depression years, many of them not to return to school at all, Cliff was learning a new and unexpected meaning of being special. It had to do with deferring dreams and bending a lively imagination to the prosaic realities of putting family solvency ahead of personal hopes. It was a hard year. But it held opportunities to learn hidden lessons about—to quote his mother Ada—making lemonade out of lemons. He returned a more mature Cliff Johnson to complete his high school senior year in 1934, the year when drought was at its worst and most of the Dakota topsoil had blown away, leaving drifts of dust that buried barbed wire fences and creating a moonscape appearance on what was previously fertile land.

Dust, drought and the Depression notwithstanding, Cliffie picked up his singing and talking ambitions with fresh vigor in the summer of 1933. He had formed a high school barbershop quartet, achieving some initial fame by appearances and school, church, and farm community entertainment events. Local farm boys showing gumption and talent with barbershop singing was a lift to farm and town folk who needed every form of morale boost possible, especially since the quartet sang without pay. Banks were foreclosing on loans, and in the early 1930's most of the rural banks in the nation were forced to close. Newspapers featured stories and pictures of soup lines for the jobless. CEO's on Michigan Avenue in Chicago were selling apples. Hopes were hard to come by, as the ranks of the unemployed grew and people went hungry. It was a testing time also for prairie preachers of the region, who offered the survival kits of prayer, courage and hope. President Franklin Delano Roosevelt had urged that the main thing to fear was fear itself, and Ada Johnson's table prayers were soft, pleading and often tearful. The Johnsons, like most farm families, had a food supply from chickens, hogs, beef and Grandma Dorothea's home-canned goods that kept the family "fed and watered" as the jargon of the 1930's put it. But it was not an obvious time to break out into song for the many who shuffled along through bone dry fields and equally arid bank holdings.

Nonetheless, The Cadets, the name chosen by the four seventeen year old quartet singers, set their sights on Chicago and the World's Fair of 1933. Young Cliff had already learned to drive a Model T Ford with its marvelous foot pedal combination for clutch, reverse, forward and the miraculous stop gears. The actual transportation was a 1929 two-door Chevrolet, on loan from sister Doris Johnson, the gifted and generous hearted school teacher and pianist who provided wheels for the Chicago-bound singers. Their send-off concert in the Beresford Veterans Hall attracted forty people, most of them relatives and friends who took up a collection of $20 and sent The Cadets off with what seemed to them a grub stake fortune. It was a daunting test for the four teenagers to drive the six hundred miles to Chicago on mostly two lane country roads that were yet to be paved.

They sang their way to the Windy City, passing the hat on street corners in every town that was a stopping place in Iowa and Illinois. One stopover at Dixon, Illinois yielded a bonanza for their harmonizing skills. Cliff helped to scribble chalk announcements on the downtown Dixon sidewalks: CONCERT TONIGHT ON COURT HOUSE LAWN, FEATURING THE FAMOUS CADET MALE QUARTET. The hat collection that night garnered six dollars and twenty cents, enough to buy bread and bologna for six well-rationed meals for several days. Just outside of Dixon an Illinois highway officer stopped them and firmly objected to the CHICAGO HERE WE COME cardboard placard placed in the back window of the Chevy. Proving they could talk as well as sing, they pleaded their way out of a state law violation and put the cardboard sign away, arriving in lonely triumph in Chicago. With remarkable bravado, Cliff drove The Cadets straight to WLS, the premier Prairie Farmer Station then located at 1230 Washington on Chicago's West Side. They talked their way into an audition and deemed it a miracle that both Harold Stafford, the program director, and the general manager George Biggars not only heard their audition but judged them good enough sing for pay at the Chicago World's Fair. It didn't hurt their attendance at all that their location was opposite the sensation of the Fair—the famous, and to some infamous, fan dancer, Sally Rand.

On one side there was the barely clad, sensuous dancer, caressing her swaying body with feather fans to the music of her style. Across the way were The Cadets belting out their hit numbers Down By The Old Mill Stream and the staple of Lutheran pietism, The Old Rugged Cross. It was a heart-stopping moment for the seventeen-year-olds when the world famous stripper blew a kiss across the way to a quartet of suddenly blushing but thoroughly fascinated Dakota clod-hoppers.

They reciprocated by sending a mixed message with their concluding number, "All Your Endearing Young Charms." In their view, at least, this was the Big Time. Not an altogether wacky conclusion. What other quartet of teenage boys from the western prairies had sung their way to Chicago, auditioned for the head people of the major radio station in the land, won approval, sang for pay at the Worlds Fair, and all this within sight and breeze distance from the feather fans of Sally Rand?

The Chicago venture bought about another stoke of good luck. The four were housed at the Chicago suburban home of the Dennis Daly family. The two-story, five-bedroom Victorian home, laced with clinging ivy vines and a huge elm tree in the front yard was a venerable landmark in the town and an elegant home away from home for the teenagers. How did four Lutheran kids from Dakota who could harmonize end up as houseguests of a Roman Catholic family? It happened because their high school history teacher in Beresford, Bessie Hemmingson, had attended college with one of the Daly girls. The old friend networking setup worked, and the boys could come home nightly from nearby temptations at the Fair to a household of hospitable Roman Catholics, a move that some Lutherans would put in the frying-pan-into-the-fire classification.

But memorable and edifying things occurred, especially at the large ground oak dinner table. It was the Daly custom to pray before the meal. One Saturday evening Mrs. Daly, with gentle feminine savvy, broke the silence and smilingly suggested "Why don't one of you say the table grace?" The seemingly forever silence that followed was finally broken by the quartet tenor, Glen Bergren, who volunteered that "Cliff could do his Norwegian prayer." Cliff froze, but this was not time to back down. With all heads bowed, and Cliff struggling for speech, Mrs. Daly again eased the awkwardness with the suggestion that all follow the family tradition of joining hands for prayer. His adrenaline starting to flow, Cliff began to pray with his bass-baritone voice barely above a whisper, then easing into his best prayer tone—

and praying the one prayer he knew—in Norwegian:

I Jesu Navin Gar Vi Til Bords, A spise Og Drikke, Pa Ditt Ored Deg Gud Til Aere, Oss Till Gavn, Sa Far Vi Mat, I Jesus Navin. Amen.

Glances from bowed heads prompted the English version:

In Jesus name to the table we go, to eat and drink, according to his word. To God, the honor, us to gain, so have we food in Jesus name. Amen.

Light, rewarding laughter moved all around the table into a memorable mealtime. Later on, when back home in South Dakota, Cliff attempted to explain to Grandma Dorothea, then 79, how he had offered a Norwegian table prayer over corned beef and cabbage in the hospitality of an Irish Roman Catholic home. She conveniently dismissed it as a joke.

The Chicago venture was more than a lark among fan dancers and Catholics. The boys discovered Chicago and experienced something of its trademark ethnic and cultural diversity. Race, color, customs, and most of all, religious worship created an ethnic ghetto comfort zone for the clusters of immigrants from Europe and elsewhere. Poles, Germans, Scandinavians, Jews, and Italians all formed their own little world community, each vocally heralding how everybody outside their own cultured heritage talked funny, wore strange clothes, and ate unpalatable food. The Chicago venture helped Cliff see his own kitchen table meals in a new light. There was no dining room in the Johnson farm home, and the children around the table were captive for firm but gentle finger-wagging sermons that were not short. It was in that setting that the stereotyping of "the other people" began to have resonance in the youthful Johnsons as well as most other families of varied ethnic strands. Sam Levinson, the Russian Jew who ran the general country store was where everyone went for food, tools, yard goods, buggy whips or cough medicine. Sam was a good businessman with bartering smarts. The Johnson family hired man, Jonas, spoke for many when stating, "He's a Jew but I like him" and saw no irony in the follow-up phrase, "Ya gotta know how to deal with him… sometimes you can even Jew him down on a price." When eleventh hour Protestant family needs surfaced it was a common, almost affectionate rural cry: "Call the Jew." Grandma Dorothea kept gently reminding the family that "these people were not our kind." Roman Catholics were congenially referred to as "Irish fish snappers," a snide label for their religious discipline of no meat served on Friday to commemorate Christ's sacrifice of himself on the cross.

What the teenage Cliff Johnson experienced in the narrowness of Dakota prairie life came back to him some eighty years later when he completed his research for his masters degree at Concordia University in River Forest, Illinois, a topic to explore later in this book. His formative years were firmly grounded—spoon fed he would sometimes agree—in Norwegian Lutheranism and Castor Oil. The two were not altogether inimical. His religious upbringing was not vicious, hate-filled, or absolutely hostile toward "the other people." It was strong, however, and cleared the system of any threats, real or perceived. Grandma Dorothea was the unofficial theological voice in the family with her ways of crafting a self-satisfying rationale for how to deal with those of another ethnic or religious tradition. "They just are not like us" was the text tailored to fit all such occasions.

But underneath the parochial limits of young Cliff Johnson's formative years there was an unspoken hunch that the veneer of piety was something of a fake as it created an ethnic, social and religious dichotomy: on the surface a cliché about "other people" but underneath it was an awareness, a curiosity and sometimes a risky attraction to someone of those "other people." An example was when the handsome young Lutheran dirt-farmer, Eric Larson, fell hopelessly in love with Roman Catholic

Bridget Riley, the testosterone prevailed. The roof fell in on both when it was discovered that she was pregnant, causing a firestorm of gossip which made eavesdropping on the party-line phones better than the soap operas on WLS.

By his eighteenth year, with his high school diploma secured, "Cliffie, you're special" had become a handed-down vision that was already taking turns and venturing down paths well distanced from its grandmotherly source. All the variations on that theme notwithstanding, however, the curly topped kid on the kitchen table now grown to his later teens, had solid underpinnings from his home and family. If those who raised him had some blinders, they had their full share of spiritual soundness and familial durability. Much of that spiritual fiber was the gift of Dorothea Olson Johnson who told him something about himself at age five that he could only know by hearing it from one he trusted for her rock-ribbed loyalty to God and love for the family. Eight decades later Cliff Johnson would recall the richness of his early years with gratitude:

> *Growing up in a family that treasured togetherness, I knew bonding and security. There, on that forty acre Dakota prairie homestead plot, my grandparents had literally carved their existence out of the grass-land earth. They stacked chunks of prairie, one upon the other, with their own hands, and over a dugout hole in the ground created a one-window sod hut. I remember that comforting feeling—all the love, hope and security with Mom, Dad, Grandma and Grandpa. The family gathering around a cob-burning blazing fired pot bellied stove, and the indescribable aroma of Grandma's home-made baked bread, loaded with sweet cream churned butter, sometimes with jelly, too. . .*

It was indeed something special at work and one more reminder of what can happen when a grandparent, or any older person for that matter, takes the time and makes the effort to tell a child something the child would never come to possess otherwise.

CHAPTER 2

You Sing Good But You Talk Better

Augustana College in Sioux Falls, South Dakota, was the next step on the way to what Cliff and his family thought was preparation for becoming a Lutheran pastor. While he had known his share of youthful chafing under the spoon-fed style of Norwegian Lutheran piety that dominated his religious upbringing, it was equally true that the family prayers, regular Sunday worship, the catechetical instruction with its strong emphasis on memorization of Scripture and Luther's Small Catechism, had become the lifelong foundation of his faith and worship. The home atmosphere, while strict in matters of faith and morals, was not without a warm-hearted love that permeated the relationships of the three generations living under one roof, providing security, affection and strength to meet the needs of life on the plains in the toughest of times. When Grandma Dorothea had delivered her "Cliffie, you're special" speech to her five-year-old grandson, which included speaking and singing so that his voice could be heard in the last row in church, it was a pastoral future that she had in mind. From time to time throughout his boyhood she would reiterate that hope in family conversations. No one proposed otherwise. A family consensus had been growing that the boy who had once stood on a cultivator seat to talk to the corn stalks would surely become the man who would stand in the pulpit and preach the Word to the congregation.

Augustana College was the ideal pre-seminary campus for Cliff to take up the curriculum that would prepare him for theological study and ordination. His first two years from 1934 - 1936 were good ones. He did well academically and continued his high school pattern of participation in extra-curricular activities. In his second year three things of decisive importance happened: he began to deliver sermonettes on the local KSOO radio station; he met the Russian Jewish immigrant station owner who gave him a sentence of advice that was life changing; and he saw an attractive brunette selling tickets in the local movie theater.

The sermonettes delivered on KSOO seemed a natural pathway toward the pastoral future. His religion professor at Augustana had encouraged him to use his rich baritone voice both for preaching and singing on the local Lutheran Hour broadcast and the fact that there was a modest stipend that went with it helped meet college expenses. Combining his interest in radio with his pre-seminary curriculum was an arrangement good enough to enable Cliff to stay on in Sioux Falls for summer school in 1934 and 1935. Within that combination, however, was a conflict he could not fully sense at the time. Was radio his future? Or was it pastoral ministry? Other circumstances soon after his third year at Augustana would provide an answer to that question.

Getting to know Joseph Henkin, the station owner, was an experience tailor made for Cliff Johnson's fascination with people, especially people who were a far cry from the Norwegian Lutheran cultural enclave of his boyhood days. Henkin's appearance was in itself a draw for the college boy who showed up at the station to sing and speak. He was not quite five-feet-five, always seemed to be seated in a cross-legged posture, rolled his own Bull Durham cigarettes, and rarely bothered to change his pongee shirt, well pockmarked with tobacco stains down the front. Joseph Henkin had found his way from the steppes of his native Russia to the Dakota plains to become something rare in that time and place, a Jewish farmer, a businessman and in 1924 the owner of radio station

KSOO. The radio station bit was symbolic of Henken's ability to follow a hunch about something new that just might have a future. He paid $250 for the station.

Gifted with a radar-like acuity in sizing up people and their best gifts, he took careful note of the collegian whose baritone voice got his attention when singing and speaking on the radio program sponsored by the Lutherans from Augustan College. He chose a propitious moment to stop by the radio station to talk with Cliff. The station was a simple affair but adequate for the times, two bedrooms and a bath on the sixth floor of the Carpenter Hotel turned into a makeshift broadcast studio. It was a Sunday. Henkin parked his 5' 4" frame into a chair, and rolled another Bull Durham cigarette, crossing his legs and cocking his head from side to side as he came directly to the point:

> *"Clifford, have you thought about postponing your ministry training for awhile, and get into this radio thing full-time?" "No" the answer came. "But I've thought about being a radio singer." "That's what I was worried about." Then came Henkin's punch line. "I've been listening to you talk and sing for a year now. You do very good. But listen to me, Clifford. You sing good but you talk better. You talk real good. Sing for fun. Not for money. Do you know what I'm talking about?" Cliff was wiggling in his chair with the force of the suggestion, but managed to blurt out "I hope I can sing, too." "You can sing," Henkin agreed, "but not make a living at it."*

That was it. You sing good but you talk better was Henkin's dictum that began to clear the air for Cliff. He had thought about a future in vocal music. Family banter and occasional joshing of friends had even suggested a career in opera. It was a lesser dream but nonetheless one among several flying around in his head. The pastoral ministry had a stronger pull on him and there was no immediate plan to drop the pre-seminary curriculum. But this brief, pithy observation about his resonant baritone voice, offered by a savvy Russian Jewish immigrant farmer-businessman, tilted him in a certain direction. What kind of speaking and in what context was as yet unknown, but a signal and been sent and received. Henkin's "You sing good but you talk better" was wise, intuitive, and prophetic, much as Grandma Dorothea's kitchen table declaration had been fifteen years earlier.

In l935, that eventful second year at Augustana, brought another key moment. The twenty year old Cliff Johnson met another twenty-year-old, Luella Marguerite Goss, the third child of Ralph and Dorthea Goss. Her father was a highly skilled wood craftsman, who counted as his masterpiece the building of the winding staircase in the Calvin Coolidge Summer White House in the Black Hills of South Dakota. She was a Sioux Falls girl, a second year student at Nettelson Business School in town, working part-time in the ticket booth at the local movie theater. Much as was Cliff, Luella had her formative beginnings in a family of solid Christian faith and practice, especially from her mother's side who made prayer and Bible study a part of the daily regimen. Hospitality was another staple of the Goss household, along with the deft handling of the less flattering side of family life. Luella absorbed these basic values derived from a strong Christian upbringing that served her later in ways that were decisive for her coming role as a wife of a husband very much in the public eye and mother of five children who would grow up in a glass house of widespread publicity. She learned early the ways to be an anchor in her own future family without becoming a drag and of making a vocation out of keeping her family and household humming under circumstances that were well out of the ordinary. Growing up under the positive influence of parents richly endowed not with money but spiritual soundness, Luella blossomed into a young woman who was bright, beautiful, unusually perceptive about people and well prepared to step into a future that would take her far from her Sioux Falls surroundings but never distant from the values she learned early and learned well.

Cliff had a room at the local YMCA. To help pay the rent he got up at 4 a.m. each morning to stoke the coal burning furnace. He also had taken the bass baritone part in Haydn's *Last Seven Words* which was scheduled to be performed at the Egyptian Theater, the movie house where Luella had her part time work in the ticket booth. Rehearsing for the concert meant more frequent theater visits, something he didn't mind at all since that meant passing by the ticket booth more frequently and a hoped-for glance at the knockout young lady working there. His hopes soared when on one occasion after a rehearsal he met her as he was walking past. "Well, hello" was her polite comment. Whatever he said in response is lost in his memory. But her greeting was enough for him to gear up his courage, don his Augustana Choir sweater with two stripes to set it off, swallow hard, and ask her to join him for a coke after work. The coke date went well, so well, in fact, that he forgot the money to pay for the coke. She paid without a murmur. The first date led to more and a romance was budding. For Cliff the excitement of falling in love with Luella set his imagination into full speed forward as he thought of every possible way to catch her fancy and mark him—once more as Grandma Dorothea had predicted—as special.

Fanciful imagination for dating gimmicks took other forms as time passed. Along with the KSOO job and stoking the furnace at the Y, he had found another part-time job to help meet college costs. Three nights a week, from 6 till 9:30 he was a go-fer at Brown's Garage. That brought three, sometimes four dollars a week. Since he was sometimes called on to drive the tow truck, he wangled permission to drive it to the theater to pick up Luella. Much to his delight, she loved being picked up at the theater in a tow truck, with a classy wave to her friends standing by as the beaming Cliff floored the accelerator and zoomed off on one of the more unusual four-wheel conveyances carrying a young pair in Sioux Falls.

But other things were happening as 1936 arrived. Cliff was at midpoint in his junior year. He was holding his own in his studies but was facing a college tuition debt that had reached $4000, a huge burden made all the more oppressive by the sixth straight year of unrelenting Depression woes. He had taken on yet another part-time job singing in the Chocolate Shop, the Greek-owned restaurant where Luella had picked up the coke tab on their first date. But the pressures of study and work brought him to another crossroads decision. Should he continue or drop out a year to regain his financial footing. School debt was the external pressure that argued for working a year and returning to finish his degree. Internally, however, another pressure was at work. It was the continuing tug of radio versus pulpit. A conversation with an Augustana faculty member helped him decide to set aside school for a year and work his way out of debt. Once again, Cliff left school and in doing so felt the subtle downdrag of that nagging epithet—dropout. But he did have a plan.

His accompanist for the restaurant singing gig, Donald Schwartz, was from LaCrosse, Wisconsin, and suggested to Cliff that the two try their luck in job hunting there. Off they went, hitch-hiking the distance, to meet a friend of Smith's, Jack Kelly, the man in charge of hiring at station WKRB. Cliff auditioned for work as a radio announcer, got it, and signed on at the station for work of any and every kind on the air, even reading menus featuring the evening specials at a local restaurant in which station owner Gerhardt Schlabach was a major stockholder. He stayed with it for six months, always with an eye on something bigger. That something bigger was KSTP in St. Paul, a major radio station in the Midwest. With a room rent debt of twenty-four dollars to deal with, he put his clothes in hock at the hotel until his planned return, and hitch-hiked the several hundred miles to Minneapolis. He came to town with five dollars in his pocket.

It was a crazy dare, but of the kind that the twenty one-year-old Johnson couldn't resist. The excitement of being behind the microphone and finding a niche in the burgeoning radio field was what he relished, and the sense was growing in him that this was his future. He auditioned at WDGY in Minneapolis, was accepted, took a room at the YMCA in St. Paul and began a "Man On The Street" program. He brought along from home his ukulele to his Sixth and Cedar Street broadcast location in St. Paul. "Do you have a favorite song?" was one opening line, useful to snag passers by for interviews, and the setup for the next line: "Tell me about you." It was people and people stories that he was after, stories of how people met their spouse, survived storms, and were making it through the Depression. It was also unique, an early form of "reality radio." The program caught on well because of Cliff's natural gift for putting people at ease who had never been on the air before. It clicked with total strangers because it was people centered, street corner and grocery store located, and without pretense in drawing out from young and old alike the things about themselves which they could not imagine were interesting enough to be aired on the radio. This was the gift he was honing, that something special of seeing what others could not see and turning it into entertainment plus motivation to pay attention to the products offered by the program sponsors.

Not every day in the Twin Cities was newsworthy, however. Thus when things needed livening up for more likely coverage, Cliff and his program partner, Jack Samuelson, put some creative imagination to work to stir up a story during National Fire Prevention Week. The Kersting Music Store was a building on the program beat. Cliff talked the building janitor into collecting some oily rags and taking them to the roof, putting a match to them, and thus "creating a little excitement" on a slow news day in the Twin Cities. The fire trucks arrived with bells and whistles full blast, and of course the Man On The Street host was there, mike in hand, to get a scoop on the downtown fire story. The fire chief was not amused when the plot was revealed that it was a fake fire. But word got around that the WDGY neophyte was a young man with a nose for news who was worth watching. He might do some unconventional things at times. But he could make things happen.

The talent behind the fake fire prank caught the attention of Kenneth Hance, program manager at KSTP, who showed enough interest in Cliff Johnson to give him an audition. Again, Cliff sailed through it successfully and soon found himself with a daily fifteen minute program plus a salary of sixty dollars a week! The pre-seminary curriculum awaiting him in his fourth year at Augustana was receding more and more into the background. The KSTP break was the big one he was hoping for, and a key development in his determination to make it with a major radio station. He was 21-years-old.

Six months into the KSTP dream job, a phone call from his sister, Doris, changed everything. "Our Joseph isn't going to make it. You'd better come home now. " It was news that stopped him in his tracks. Joseph Johnson was his younger brother, a bright, six foot lad, well gifted and prized as the youngest child in the family. At age fifteen he had been stricken suddenly with a kidney disease that could have been remedied with two shots of penicillin had it existed in those pre-wonder drug days. A decision had to be made immediately and Cliff struggled with it. To be a rising radio star personality at a station of the stature of KSTP was a rare plum. Brooks Henderson, a staple in the radio field, was interested in the position Cliff was creating and actively competed for it. Cliff took his heartache to the station manager, Kenneth Hance, who gave him the counsel and the encouragement that helped him do the right thing. A younger brother stricken with an ominous disease was the clear priority. With Kenneth Hance's permission and blessing, he left KSTP and all it portended, and returned home to join the family vigil of care for Joseph. Cliff worked out a system whereby he took an announcer job back at KSOO in Sioux Falls, where Mr. Henkin had told him to put speaking over singing. He could commute by bus or hitch hike the seventy five mile round-trip to Beresford and his brother's bedside with regularity, singing and speaking and praying with him. By mid-December, 1937, the end came for Joseph Johnson. With the whole family gathered at the hospital room bedside, the commendation was spoken: "Lord, we now commit Joseph to you…"

Only those who have passed through such a loss know the depth of grief that comes with the death of a boy with so many gifts and so much ahead of him. The family grieved for Joseph. For Cliff it was not only the grief for a younger brother lost to an untimely death. It meant revisiting the old struggle of whether he should return to Augustana and become a pastor after all. That conflict was not resolved and the wounds of Joseph's death rubbed it raw once again. The KSTP experience had been powerful and positive, a strong draw toward a radio career. The untimely illness and death of Joseph put the pastoral vocation back on the horizon, with a pull on his conscience that made it somehow a choice that would compensate for a lost brother. Joseph and Ada Johnson were wise enough parents not to dictate his future course. They had enough on their hands with the ongoing battle against drought, dust, hail and an economy that was all but shot. As tough a year as 1938 was for the Johnsons, Cliff, and countless others in the land, it was nonetheless the year of a premier event in Cliff's life.

He married Luella Marguerite Goss.

The day was July 12. The place was First Lutheran Church in Sioux Falls. The temperature was 112 degrees, with a humidity reading of 80 percent. South Dakotans had to abide such heat when planning mid-summer weddings, knowing that the only relief in church came from the fans supplied by the local funeral homes. It was uncommon that Cliff's Norwegian Lutheran Synod pastor and Luella's Missouri Synod Lutheran pastor of German heritage joined in conducting the wedding service. The rule was that the two Lutheran groups stayed separate in worship and practice for reasons that only the clergy could explain. But a wedding brought together two staunch families from each tradition and the clergy did not object.

The main reason to forget the temperature was Luella, gorgeous in her wedding gown. Her face was radiant, even more stunning than when

Cliff first laid eyes on her at the theater booth, and no 112 degree heat could diminish her stunning beauty. Cliff noted that she wore flat-soled shoes since she was an inch taller than he. Over the next fifty five years her frequent and gentle reminder to him was "Don't slump. Stand up straight!" And for the next five and one half decades he did, finding in her good reason to stand tall in more ways than posture.

The wedding went off without a hitch, due in no small part to the planning and help of Luella's sister, Myrna. No fainting. No heat stroke. Fans aplenty to keep the stifling air circulating around the sanctuary. The reception was held at a beautiful vintage Victorian home, converted for this and other community purposes. Everyone from both families attended, of course, as well as a wide circle of friends from near and far. Colleagues from Radio Station KSOO and the Egyptian Theater were on hand to provide name tags, tend to the punch bowl, and keep busy in "playing tricks"—in the jargon of the times—that were part of every wedding reception. In refilling the punch bowl as needed, guests began to note an unusual, delightfully pungent taste. Cliff's mother whispered in her son's ear that "Reverend Stephan is looking strange and his wife says he is mumbling like a drinker." She was right. In fact, even the children were talking louder than unusual and getting out of hand. Then George Rohn from the radio station abruptly grabbed up the punch bowl and emptied it into the bathroom water closet. In no time all the guests knew why. Another guest from KSOO, radio engineer Gene Dennis had poured a pint of gin into the punch bowl. Aunt Marie, not given to humor at the thought of punch well spiked with gin, harrumphed that the trick players were "the devil's servants." Everyone else, however, took it in the spirit of fun and good humor and got home safely.

The reception ended but there was still one trick remaining. An Augustana College classmate, Lee Wangsnesss, kept a straight face while informing Cliff that Cliff's 1930 Chevy, parked and ready for the honeymoon trip, had mysteriously turned up with a flat tire. What Cliff found, however, when hurrying to the car, was that Joseph Henkin, cherished mentor and station boss at KSOO, had ordered the garage to put on four new tires, tune it and fill the gas tank. Not a small item for a young couple just starting out for Minneapolis. It was not the only class act from Joseph Henkin. He had booked a handsome suite for the Johnsons at the Radisson Hotel in Minneapolis, in exchange, to be sure, for some commercials that Cliff had recorded beforehand. A suite at the Radisson was a rare treat, since the couple arrived at the upscale hotel with seven dollars between them. This was an era when many a bride had a one word answer to the question of where she and her groom honeymooned: "upstairs." The Radisson was extraordinary, as was the exceptional man that made it possible.

Detroit Lakes and the lovely summer home of Luella's sister, Myna, was their next stop. So captured was Cliff by the lake, the water, a row boat and a fishing pole, that he soon stripped down to his shorts and was out on the lake fishing for three hours. That evening at supper the severe sunburn began to set in. He was faint and excused himself, blisters popping out all over his body. Luella and Myrna wanted him in the hospital, calling the doctor with that in mind. But Cliff, miserable though he was, regarded a honeymoon in the hospital as more miserable still and didn't go. Swabbed with applications of vinegar towel pads for the next four hours and through the night, the fair-skinned and now parboiled Norwegian bridegroom recovered enough to barely turn over in bed. It was grist for family humor for years afterward, how Cliff and Luella spent some of their honeymoon in twin beds.

In October the newlyweds moved to Lincoln, Nebraska, where Luella quickly found an ad taking job for a trade paper at twelve dollars a week. Cliff had made the grade in an interview for a radio job with Judson Woods, program manager at Central States Network, a combination of three stations that covered a range of several hundred miles around Lincoln. His job was exactly the kind that appealed to him and where his talents served him best, creating new programs that blended stories of such vivid past events as the Great Blizzard of 1888 with interview programming that spoke directly to the main thing on peoples' minds at the time—getting work and holding onto jobs. Cliff knew enough about blizzards and tornadoes from his boyhood days to make such programming not only listenable but also a reminder that in new and encouraging ways the pioneer legacy of surviving the worst held lessons of durability through the hard times of the present. His interviews with people of the daily rounds were purposely slanted toward good news for the huge number of job-seekers who tuned in. "Emma Harms got her job yesterday!" was typical of his way of putting a face on the anonymity of hard times. He thought up the idea of taking the microphone to building sites, interviewing workmen putting up a new house, advertising the contractors who welcomed the publicity, and above all, providing hope for listeners that the day might come when "Building A Dream house" programming would air the story of their own dreams coming true. The script was a commercial bonanza. Sponsors were not hard to find for such hands-on programming that publicized their products and services while stirring hopes in the minds of listeners who would use them. It was a good turn of events for Cliff and Luella. With her twelve dollars a week and his forty dollars a week, they could meet the rent on their house, put groceries on the table and gain confidence that they were a team well suited in working together toward a promising future.

It is important to realize the power of radio as a prime medium in the America of the late 1930's. What had begun with the first commercial broadcast in 1920 had mushroomed to a nationwide phenomenon in just two decades. The Atwater Kent table model was a fixture in countless homes, and if one family couldn't afford a set it was a neighborly commonplace to invite others over to listen to events like the Joe Louis knockout of Max Schmeling or Ma Perkins, Vic and Sade, and other daytime soap opera staples, plus the evening program favorites such as the Lux Radio Theater and Amos and Andy. Radio brought at least temporary respite from the Depression doldrums with its invitation to gather the family and/or neighbors and tune in programming that offered another world of fantasy, humor and relief from the constant worries of making it in a hard-scrabble world. In the more localized region in and around Lincoln and Omaha Nebraska, Cliff Johnson helped make that happen.

Radio's imaginative world could stir Cliff's own natural gift for spotting a new idea and running with it. One evening, as Luella was preparing supper, Cliff was listening to the George Burns and Gracie Allen Show from Hollywood. It was a prime-time program, immensely popular from coast-to-coast. Gracie announced her zany idea of running for president. George, the consummate straight man, poured cold water on the idea with his common-sense put-down that housewives don't cook up a campaign out of the blue and go on the stump. As George elaborated on his presidential campaign wisdom, he mentioned among other things that Gracie "would have to get a midwest base for the necessary popular vote—someplace in the heartland like…Nebraska!" The throwaway line brought Cliff bolt upright on the couch and immediately set him to thinking out loud about a scenario that the Burns-Allen line had stirred in his imagination. "We'll get Burns and Allen to Omaha…turn out the town to meet them…set up a mock campaign…do it all, have fun at it, and make Nebraska Gracie's first stop on her run for the White House…" It was, of course, as realistically imaginative as Gracie's own presidential run was pure fancy. And it was vintage Cliff Johnson.

The next mooring he went to his boss and general manager at KOIL, Don Searle, who had also heard the program. Searle caught the spirit of Cliff's idea and convinced others, including the initially reluctant mayor, Daniel R. Butler to join in, secure sponsors, and make the case to George Burns and Gracie Allen in Hollywood. Ben Burns, George's brother, was the key person in making the contact. A previously planned Golden Spike Ceremony in Omaha, commemorating the centennial of the completing of the transcontinental railroad, was co-opted to help provide funding for Gracie's campaign kickoff spoof. Men in Omaha were already growing beards and women were outfitting themselves in dresses of a century ago. The mammoth AKSARBEN convention hall, built by Chicagoan William Wirtz, was engaged and the Omaha World Herald promised full coverage. The Burns-Allen idea had pumped considerably more energy into what had been envisioned as a civic event, and in the huge crowd that turned out to witness the arrival of George and Gracie, their whole entourage, plus Ray Noble and his orchestra was a young Nebraskan whose interest in such entertainers would lead to a notable future of his own. His name was Johnny Carson.

The radio star guests were welcomed royally and treated to a parade down Omaha's Main Street. Waving from their convertible as the irrepressible Gracie tossed out "Gracie For President" buttons to onlookers lining the street and half-wondering if Gracie wouldn't be a plus in the White House after all. Throughout the week the hoopla continued, much to the delight of the Omaha elite, the sponsors, the people from in and beyond the city, and no less to Cliff Johnson in whose head the whole event had been concocted and carried through. It gave him confidence that spur of the moment ideas might just take off if timing, content and collaboration were all in place, and it convinced Luella that her second-guessing of supper hour inspirations by her husband might deserve a second thought. Along with the confidence-building effect of the week was something more substantial for Cliff. He had found a way to sit in on scripting sessions that week with Burns and Allen and their writers and program people. It was comedy with an emotional ring that he detected as the key to their nationwide following. George wrote the one-liners, Cliff noted, and had the last word on what made it to the program and what was cut. Gracie was the comedy genius, the first woman to be so regarded in the radio world, but it was George who was in charge of everything. In watching how a program was developed, Cliff took note of George Burns' sense of the crisis background against which people listened, not only the crisis of Depression-weary times in America but as a Jew with his eye on the wider world of ominous signs emerging from Nazi Germany and Adolph Hitler's venomous diatribes against Jews world-wide. A final touch to the triumph of the week was Cliff's remembering that Gracie Allen had a fondness for teddy bears. He sent a supply to her room with a message of gratitude for the week. She responded with an invitation for Cliff and Luella to join them at their Continental Hotel suite for a private dinner. The experience helped revise their starstruck image of the two radio superstars. Cliff recalled that the conversation was mainly about family, with the Burns couple inquiring graciously about the South Dakota roots of Cliff and Luella.

If Cliff was tempted to soar a bit too high from the Burns-Allen success, he was brought abruptly to earth by an Omaha airport interview with another Hollywood personality who had come to town for an appearance. Orson Welles was riding high on his 1938 "War Of The Worlds" radio broadcast in which he had shaken up millions of Americans who heard his stentorian voice announce the coming of hostile invaders from outer space. One of the sensations of the year and a reminder of how powerful a medium radio could be. Cliff Johnson had heard that program while driving home to Omaha from an assignment out of town, and arranged to meet the DC3 as Welles stepped from the plane. After questions about the impact of the outer-space invasion program, he asked Orson Welles about the gossip that he was chasing Dolores Del Rio all over Hollywood, fishing for something lively to add to the rumor mill. "It's none of your damn business" was the curt retort and the interview was over. Johnson learned something from the put-down, principally that an interviewer lets the interviewee lead the course of the conversation. He learned also that there was an unspoken code of respectful avoidance of the darker side of prominent people. That code was in effect in the radio world of the 1930's, but it's future was short lived as later decades of radio talk shows and reality television drew primarily from the darker side of human nature, seeking to turn it into entertainment.

From l938 till l941, his longest stay at one radio job to date, Cliff enjoyed solid gain in his burgeoning radio career. He wrote and hosted programs that reflected his primary talent for relating to people from all walks of life. In an interview with Glenn Miller, who rose to national fame with his new and velvet smooth sounds on the Big Band scene, the interview centered on Miller's rise to the top in entertainment notoriety as much as feature his humble beginnings in Clarinda, Iowa. The band leader who had put *Moonlight Serenade, In the Mood, The Five O'Clock Whistle* and *I Gotta Gal in Kalamazoo* into the record collections of millions of teenagers had come to Omaha in l939, just as his career was taking off. He spoke, however, of the death of his parents and how that loss affected him, his marriage, and his first try at a musical instrument—the mandolin. Cliff could relate well to Miller's flunking out of college, since his own drop-out baggage was still with him. So it was not Glenn Miller the pop music idol that emerged from the interview, but Glenn Miller the man who had come from modest beginnings, who knew heartache and failure, and who—unknown at interview time—would lose his life a few years later over the English Channel in World War II.

The l939 movie hit, "Boys Town" brought the two stars, Spencer Tracey and Mickey Rooney to Omaha for the premier showing. Cliff was there, mike in hand, and the interview went well. More important, however, was the growing contact and friendship with Father Edward Flanagan, the legendary priest and founder of Boys Town which was a haven for kids with no family. Cliff had come to know Fr. Flanagan from other interviews in connection with Boys Town Choir concerts and other civic events in which the priest and his work were featured. On one occasion in l940 Cliff was sitting in Flanagan's office talking with him about his future. Out of the blue, Flanagan sat back in his chair, fixed a savvy eye on Johnson, and said what he thought: "Cliffie, you ought to be up there with the big boys." Up there meant Chicago. The big boys were not the station personnel at KOIL Omaha, but the CBS radio people of WBBM in Chicago. The statement startled young Cliff, but immediately set his heart pounding. It was another one of those prophetic moments of the order of Grandma Dorothea in the South Dakota farm kitchen and Joseph Henkin in the KSOO studio in Sioux Falls. Whatever more was said is not remembered; Cliff was too awed, scared, eager and incredulous to remember more of the moment, except that Father Edward Flanagan picked up his telephone, got through to Bobby Brown of WBBM in Chicago, and arranged for Cliff to send him a sample tape of his radio work. The tape was made and sent. The result was an approval by WBBM for an audition. As soon as he could get to Chicago, he made the trip, met Brown, the program manager, and Les Atlas, WBBM owner. In 1933 Cliff and The Cadets had breezed their way into the same studio for a break to sing at the World's Fair. Now, eight years later, he was back in more promising circumstances. His voice and radio style clicked. He was in the big leagues of national radio, the nerve center for producing and airing the immensely popular soap operas that held the fascination of the nation. With Luella and a lively one-year-old daughter, he arrived in Chicago, thrilled to have the opportunity given him and pleased to begin work at the considerable salary of $70 a week.

He was now 25. Already he was a veteran of a half dozen radio positions and locations, his imagination buoyed by career successes, his inward character tested by the death of a kid brother, his wife and young family an anchor of inspiration and needed grounding for his imagination and energy. He reported for work at 5:30 each morning, went over plans with station announcers for the programming of the day which began at 6 a.m. and put his talents to work in programming and announcing that helped him grow in the world of radio at its peak. He was sold on the power of the human voice to project images in the minds of listeners more vividly and lasting than the television screen that was soon to replace radio's supremacy in American life. But radio could do then what it still does now, transmit well-spoken words through the air, stirring human imagination to envision stories and scenarios that are unrivaled by any man-made screen.

CHAPTER 3

Up There With The Big Boys

anding a prize job at WBBM was a huge break, one that catapulted Cliff Johnson to the top echelons of the Chicago radio world. The CBS affiliate joined three other stations, WLS (the call letters stood for World's Largest Store, the modest claim of its first owner, Sears Roebuck Company), WGN (World's Greatest Newspaper, as its Chicago Tribune owner reminded listeners), and WMAQ, it ranked among the strongest stations anywhere in the nation. The soap opera world emanated from its studios. Ma Perkins, Vic and Sade, and other daytime favorites were the daily fare of millions of Americans. Housewives phoned each other to chat over episodes. Office workers would take long lunch breaks, even come home over the lunch hour when possible, so as not to miss another chapter in the story. Getting on board at WBBM was the dream for which every aspiring young announcer or script writer would give his eye teeth.

He was "up there with the big boys" in Father Flanagan's provocative phrase. The big boys lineup included Les Atlas, Fran Allison, Dale Evans, Bobby Brown, Jim Conway, Fahey Flynn, John Harrington, Tommy Bartlett, Les Paul and others who had made it into this charmed circle. Radio was at its peak in the nation. From Chicago came the radio signals that crisscrossed the Midwest and beyond. For a rookie from the Dakota prairie to go on the air at this level was unprecedented. To stand before a microphone and announce "This is the WBBM Radio Theater, Wrigley Building, Chicago" gave him a spine-tingling thrill at the thought of listeners tuning in from dozens of surrounding states and as far beyond as Alaska.

How was it that Cliff Johnson got the nod?

One part of the answer is Les Atlas, the WBBM owner and general manager who hired him. He was a marketing genius with a canny sense for knowing how to find talent in unlikely places for programming that would attract and hold the interest of women—the primary listeners during the daylight hours. He and his brother were radio pioneers in the 1920's who worked their way up from their hometown roots in Lincoln, Illinois. That background gave Atlas a feel for the kind of programming that would draw listeners from the heartland. He took over the fledgling WBBM when coming to Chicago in 1930. By 1940 his programming vision and gutsy sense for finding talent had produced a trio of young comers, just on the cusp of emerging stardom.

He helped put Les Paul on the map, a country music string-picking guitar player from Waukesha, Wisconsin, with the unlikely nickname of Rhubarb Red. He pioneered the electronic guitar sound that has become the country music sound signature that we know. Cliff's first program with Les Paul was memorable. The CBS and Wrigley front office people had cooked up a deal with head trainer Andy Lotshaw of the Chicago Cubs to promote "The Andy Lotshaw Body Rub" a creamy lather concoction famous for rub downs. Cliff had to keep a straight face when announcing "Hello out there, from CBS in Chicago, here is Rhubarb Red, Les Paul, with his own inimitable variations on My Darling Clementine, brought to you by Andy Lotshaw's Body Rub." It was a mouthful at the time. No one but Les Atlas might have guessed that the Andy Lotshaw sponsored Rhubarb Red's original Gibson hand-made guitar would one day find a place of honor in the Smithsonian Institute or that the people of Waukesha, Wisconsin, would erect a three-story museum housing the many cherished instruments and inventions of their native son.

Cliff Johnson became a friend of another Les Atlas talent discovery, Fran Allison, of Kukla, Fran and Ollie puppet fame. She was a fourth grade school teacher from Pocahontas, Iowa, with a good singing voice and a flair for story-telling. She had been drawn to radio as a promising channel for using her talents and started her new career at WOC in Davenport, Iowa, where a young radio announcer named Ronald Reagan was on his way up the ladder. Encouraged by her early success behind a microphone, she auditioned at WBBM in Chicago where Les Atlas was quick to recognize her talent. A serious car accident left her with severe facial injuries which were only partially removed through reconstructive surgery that was remarkable for its time. During her long recovery, and due to her shyness over her appearance, she virtually hid behind the microphone and developed the puppeteer talents that became her trademark later on. Among the first scripts Cliff produced at WBBM featured Fran Allison. On the morning it was to air, the script was nowhere to be found and Cliff was sweating out the fact that he was the one who had lost it. Allison handled the dilemma with nonchalance and relished the challenge of ad-libbing the entire program with Cliff. The two took off in lively exchanges that were better, not worse, for having no manuscript to follow. This was something unknown at WBBM where every word had to be written, polished, and approved beforehand. The result was beneficial for both. New doors of broadcast opportunity opened for her. For Cliff it meant a promotion to a seven day a week program schedule and a salary boost to $110 a week. Cliff's wife, Luella, was also part of a warm friendship that developed. Allison was a next door neighbor to the Johnsons on Chicago's north side. Both women shared common ground as daughters of families with strong religious roots which nurtured prayer and integrity as essentials in daily life.

Dale Evans was the third person in the stable of WBBM talent on the way up. Les Atlas had brought her to Chicago from Texas where she had begun as a country singer. She became a friend of Cliff's and needed solid friendship to stabilize her life after two broken marriages. The healing influence of friendship with Cliff helped prepare her for what followed, meeting and marrying Roy Rogers and a marriage of more than fifty years that led them both to movie and television fame.

It was extraordinary, then, for Cliff to become the latest addition to a WBBM talent pool that was a commentary on Les Atlas' signature line when spotting people of promise, "We can smell the meat a'cookin'." Atlas, respectfully known around the station as "The Skipper" or "The Old Man" but never on a first name basis with anyone, wanted to fill a particular niche for which Cliff Johnson was uniquely suited. He could reach a woman's audience.

Every station program director in the land knew that women made up the vast majority of daytime radio listeners. The question was how to reach them. Other major stations played records, counted on soap opera, and fed in other features designed to interest women. Atlas saw something unique in Johnson's best characteristic, a people-centered interviewer with creative ideas for talking with, not at, women and doing it with an ease and warmth that could make first-timers on the air comfortable.

Timing and luck also played into the factors which influenced Les Atlas to move Johnson into a plum position at WBBM. An earlier program host for reaching a woman's audience was another Atlas pick who made good at big city radio from small town beginnings. Tommy Bartlett had brought with him from Wisconsin a distinctive style, an early version of Jackie Gleason, both in one-liner quips for quick laughs and a generous girth. He had gained a following on the "Meet The Missus" and "Shopping With The Missus" programs. As contract renewal time came around late in 1941, Bartlett abruptly left the station to join the service as a military transport pilot. To fill the opening, Atlas sought a successor

but not a carbon copy of Bartlett. He saw in Johnson not a rotund quip-
ster but a skinny communicator who could create two-way radio conversations with women that helped them discover that they were interesting
in themselves and not simply a foil for the star quality of the host. This
was the Johnson trademark. He was people-centered. His man-on-the-
street style clicked with people from all walks of life, ranging from the
mega-stars George and Gracie Burns to the Omaha housewife who got
her job back one day. Atlas spotted it and put Johnson to work as host of
several programs for which he was ideally suited.

His typical format seemed almost too simple. His "Do You Know The
Answer" program aired at 8:15 a.m. daily. The hour when housewives listened with one ear while tuning the other toward the sounds of kids
going out the door for school. Cliff had a pool of a hundred or more
names and phone numbers of people he would call at random. His opening line was a cheery "This is Cliff 'Twenty-Five-Dollar-In-The-Pocket'
Johnson" followed by a plug for the program sponsor, Tip Top Bread.
The Tip Top wrapper, he would explain, had a cluster of stars at the end
and the question was to guess how many stars. The twenty five dollar
prize for the right answer was nothing to sneeze at in 1941, and then the
radio banter would move on to things of interest to women. The program
was a statement that the lives and opinions of housewives mattered. They
were not merely used as consumers but valued as persons with something
to say, not earthshaking in every instance but still listenable and capable
of worthwhile morning conversation.

His "Listen To Cliff" program, which he launched late in 1941, aired
from 7:30 - 8:15 a.m. daily and soon established him as a household
name throughout the WBBM listening audience. He learned this one
morning when a delayed start from home meant he was pushing 70 mph
down Chicago's Marine Drive to the Wrigley Building. The police officer
who pulled him over asked him where he was going in such a rush and
who did he think he was. The response was a humble but effective,

"I'm Cliff Johnson and I've got to be on the air at the Wrigley Building in twelve minutes." With that, the officer snapped his traffic ticket book shut, nodded his head in affirmation that he knew that voice from somewhere, and gave the terse command: "Follow me." The two made it to the studio in time. Cliff did not miss the opportunity to make the Chicago Police officer his first radio guest of the day, only grateful to have been stopped by a radio fan who knew his voice instantly and was happy, if not somewhat awed, to find himself as the first Chicago cop ever to swap a fat traffic fine for an interview on a major radio station.

The "Listen To Cliff" program popularity was built on impromptu contacts with people from all walks of life, and again it was primarily women who were heard from via the letters they wrote in and the stories they told. The Johnson touch was consistent: in addressing people talking to them one person at a time rather than addressing an impersonal mass. Letters typically told of household and family events. He would pick up on those with some particular appeal, reach the writer by phone on the air, and get right at a subject bound to catch women's interests. A typical opener was to greet the housewife by name and ask what dress she was wearing today. A reply might be, "One with polka dots." The Johnson comeback would be…"How many polka dots would you guess?" If the answer would be a stab in the dark it didn't matter. It was a subject to pick up and go with, and when Johnson sensed that the interviewee was coming up with prize-worthy answers he would clinch the banter with the announcement that a check for twenty-five dollars was on its way. Another response he often received when inquiring about what the plans of the day might include was a favorite: "I'm having my hair fixed today!" After a decade of slim household finances during the Depression, the thought of going out for a beauty shop visit was a sure-fire winner, and Johnson was skilled to take such commonplace leads and turn them into dialog on family and neighborhood interests that kept thousands of other women listeners attentive. Occasionally included celebrity guests, but the strength of the program was lively, consistent attention to people with whom a widespread audience could readily identify. That was what Les Atlas was looking for. That was what Cliff Johnson supplied and why he got the position.

One memorable morning in April, 1941, he was again cruising to work along Chicago's outer drive that borders Lake Michigan, this time well within the speed limits. His nineteen-month-old curly top daughter, Sandra, was with him in his pearl gray LaSalle Cadillac, relentlessly pressing him with queries about where they were going and why. Luella was ill that morning. There was no baby-sitter alternative to taking her along to the studio. Arriving at the second floor studios at the Wrigley Building, he checked in for his morning work of hosting "Do You Know The Answer?" Walking into a WBBM studio with a toddler made the broadcast crew instantly dubious. This had not happened before. Cliff propped his toddler up on two Chicago phone directories and started his "This is Cliff, twenty-five-dollars-in-the-pocket" routine. Sandra, quiet as a mouse at first, piped up with a very audible "Daddy, Daddy, Daddy…" Cliff backpedaled expertly, filling in the audience with the news that "this is my daughter, and this is a day off for my wife, Luella." Hoping it would suffice, he added "Look, dear, just wait till I finish the program." It didn't suffice. Sandra countered with "Daddy, Daddy, I can't." Cliff pleaded, "Please, dear." Sandra's ultimatum followed, "Daddy, I can't. I HAVE TO GO."

The mild consternation that erupted from the studio crew was indicative of the radio culture of the early 1940's in which nobody knew what to do with that on-air statement never found in any script. Cliff handled it as any Dad would. He took her to the bathroom, and then, as he later confessed to Luella, tried to disappear. The impromptu call of nature and Cliff's paternal response made him worry that he would lose his job. He came to work the next morning wondering what awaited him, but was surprised and relieved to learn that the WBBM switchboard had already lit up with approving calls from delighted listeners. "Who is that child?" and "Keep the kid on—she livens up a dull show" were among the responses that planted the seed of an idea in Johnson's mind. Six years later Sandra and her siblings were kids on the air around the Johnson family breakfast table in a program destined to run for ten years as a first of its kind on a national radio network. Sandra's serendipitous moment hinted at the power of a child's voice, free and unrehearsed, to say what kids say, when they choose to say it, and reveal how well it could go over with a radio audience. Cliff caught the hint and stored it away.

Johnson's radio style and voice was developing a credibility that subtly communicated the message that the commonplaces and daily rounds in the lives of wives, mothers, and grandmothers truly mattered. It wasn't trivia. It was life as millions of women lived it, women who had weathered the worst Depression in America's history and now were facing the threat of another world war. Sooner than they would ever wish, the women of America were not only sending their sons and husbands off to war but were themselves leaving the home to take on new "Rosie the Riveter" roles that were essential to the defense industry and thus to the war's outcome.

Did Les Atlas have instincts that could probe that far into the murky future? Did Cliff himself sense something of the new ways that would soon lift the role of women to new levels? These intangibles could not be measured. What could be measured was the increasingly healthy bottom line as Cliff took over "Meet the Missus" and "Shopping With The Missus" programs. This was an era well before Nielsen Ratings and Sweep Weeks determined the shelf life of programs, but the readiness of companies to come on board as sponsors was not lost on Les Atlas and the CBS corporate leadership. Businesses wanted in on programming that reached into a market dominated by the women who were the primary purchasers of their products.

All of this came at a whirlwind pace for Cliff. As a naturally gifted 26-year-old, was he up to the pressures of not only getting a dream job but holding it day in and day out? The work was demanding. He would sign in at the station at 5:30 a.m., to begin the work day by going over scheduled programming and editing scripts before they were on the air. While he could admit to an edge of nervousness before air time, he worked hard at preparation and made it his business to do what all radio professionals did, warm up the audience before the red light came one. That audience contact inevitably put nervousness aside as the adrenaline kicked in. He was fully immersed in what he was doing and loved the dynamic of interacting with people, both visible in the studio audience as well as with the vast listening audience he could only envision. It was no less so for Luella. She had her hands full in 1941 as a housewife with an eighteen month old daughter to care for. With her intelligence and empathetic encouragement she was steadily there for her husband, providing frequent ballast for his dreams and helping him distinguish them from pipe dreams.

In the short span of a half dozen years Cliff had moved from a Sioux Falls, South Dakota, sixth floor makeshift radio studio in the Carpenter Hotel to the sparkling white-granite prominence of the Wrigley Building on Chicago's Michigan Avenue. It was a rarified atmosphere into which he was settling, to be sure. He seemed born to it. Father Flanagan had aptly named it as being "up there with the big boys." He had arrived.

Something else arrived late in 1941 that would affect Cliff, the nation, and the world. On December 7th, the Japanese attacked Pearl Harbor and the United States was jolted out of an isolation that kept at a distance Hitler's ravaging of Europe and Japan's choke hold on East Asia. On December 8th the congress declared war; the country was stunned by a sneak attack that, in President Franklin Roosevelt's memorable phrase, would live on as a day of infamy. All across the land young men were enlisting military service as volunteers or draftees.

As his radio career flourished at WBBM, it also collided with his conscience.

He was living in comfort, had a dream job, and was driving a Cadillac to and from work. As the spring of 1942 passed, he marked his 27th birthday and could not help noticing with increasing discomfort the numbers of men going off to war, some from the studio, some from his circle of friends and some from his family. The internal conflict burdened him. He talked with Luella about it. She could understand but could not agree that his best move was to leave her, his two children, his work, and the meteoric career that was growing more promising by the day. Finally, on October 14, 1942, he put the instinct of his heart over the logic in his head and went to the recruiting office of the United States Navy located on the second floor of a building at 4700 N. Broadway. He reached the stop step of the stairway, hesitated, turned and walked back down to street level, momentarily stymied by a tug-of-war inside his heart and mind. One side of the struggle centered on Luella and her strong conviction that a 27-year-old husband and father of two young children was not subject to the draft, as well as Les Atlas' not too subtle reluctance to lose another key radio personality to the war effort. On the other was the sense of duty, the action of colleagues who had signed up, the daily sight of more and more young men enlisting and the general atmosphere of a national fervor to withstand enemies that clearly threatened the future of the United States. On an October day in 1942 he decided to take his U.S. Navy enlistment papers to the draft board office at 4700 N. Broadway to inform them. He walked up the stairs to the second floor office, thought about it one more time, and walked back down the stairs to the street where he agonized a full half hour over what to do. Finally he returned up the stairs and this time made it to the draft board door, showed them his papers and headed straight downtown for the first of two ceremonies of enlistment in the Navy. That evening at the supper table, when the meal was finished, he cleared his voice, worked up his courage, and announced his action to Luella. It was greeted with silent acceptance but no enthusiasm. Similarly, when he went on to tell her that he had received a raised-eyebrow response at the draft board "You, a 27-year-old and father of two…enlisted?" it did little for his confidence that he had made the right decision. It tested his resolve as it well should be tested. It was not a drama unique to him.

He was one of thousands of young American men who soon discovered the chasm between the idealism of thinking about signing up to serve the country and what happened when reality set in. At the Great Lakes Naval Station, just north of Chicago, he got a dose of what GI meant. His government issue haircut left nothing on his head but his bare scalp. He was stripped naked, exchanging his civvies for Navy gear that was thrown at him, together with shoes that didn't fit. The Chief Petty Officer in charge fit the image of the CPO who could swear like a sailor. Then and there it hit him. At one moment he was the civilian husband, father of two small children, well dressed and well employed. The next moment he was a serial number, naked as a jay-bird, stripped of all dignity and self-esteem as well, humiliated and brainwashed, angry and crying as though a convicted criminal. Loaded up with a full pack of Navy gear on his back and trudging the mile long trek at Navy Pier in Chicago, a thought hit him hard. What moral and ethical route could he take to get out of the Navy! He was vulnerable and felt a bone-deep apprehension, not a fear born of cowardice but one born of having no control over anything. He was in the Navy now, and it wasn't something to sing about.

As his boot training at Great Lakes ended, he was assigned to a unit scheduled for active duty in the South Pacific where momentous naval battles with the Japanese were beginning to turn the tide toward hope for an American victory in the Pacific war. He had no problem with being in the navy and was prepared to serve where assigned. But he did have a problem with killing people, a dilemma he never fully resolved during his nearly three year tour-of-duty. As the orders came to ship out, he put through a phone call to Chaplain Hjalmar Hansen, the director of the Great Lakes Naval Choir under whom Cliff had sung. During the conversation in which he thanked Hansen for the experience of singing under him, Hansen asked him for his serial number. The phone conversation ended. But before Johnson was shipped out for the South Pacific, Hansen called back. He had immediately gone to work requesting Johnson's reassignment which would keep him stateside with duty commensurate with his particular talent and experience.

It was an enormously welcome turn of events. He was assigned to a ship-company billet at Great Lakes. Some time after he chanced to meet the CPO who had thrown the navy gear and shoes at him and whose purple language had disgusted him. To Cliff's amazement, the man had attended a concert of the Blue Jacket Choir and recognized him as a soloist. The CPO complimented him with a surprise comment that reversed the well-remembered Henkin line about singing good but talking better. "Heard your solo with the choir last night. You sing pretty good!" Johnson, in no mood for compliments from that source, turned and walked away. But there was something in the crusty petty officer's tone that resonated with Cliff. He was a regular now and no longer a reserve. He was under orders and could not call the shots. The thought even came to him as he mused over the comment that he might learn to like the guy. The Navy wasn't WBBM. Around him was a whole new cast of characters with whom he had to learn to get along. His horizons on human nature, including his own, were expanding in ways he had not expected. He wasn't up there with the big boys, but out there among a boot camp full of strangers dressed in Navy blue.

Meanwhile Luella was bracing herself for what turned out to be her thirty two month stretch as a Navy wife. She agreed with Cliff's urging to go to live with her family in South Dakota and dutifully packed up daughters Sandy and Pamela and the household belongings for the trip back to Sioux Falls. It was not easy to move in with her parents, take up her old cashier job at the Egyptian Theater ticket booth, and be hundreds of miles away from her husband. She was but one among several million young American women, however, who were experiencing in their own realm the realities of wartime life.

As a Navy specialist in writing and producing scripts for military use, First Class non-commissioned officer Clifford Tilman Johnson was sent to Cleveland, Ohio. He was assigned additional work in naval photography and had the good fortune of training under Lieutenant Mike Milligan, a former photographer from the Chicago Tribune. In two weekends of instruction under Milligan, he learned the right mix of chemicals for developing film and soon progressed to having a lab assigned to him for his work. He wrote materials for the Navy brass, sang in the naval choir, and tried his hand at composing. His "Dress Blues" made it on a national NBC network broadcast. He worked on Navy radio programs with a young Durwood Kirby, who later achieved broadcast fame with Gary Moore and Arlene Francis on "What's My Line?" A welcome turn of events came in 1944 when Luella and the girls were able to join him. They found a house at a charming location in the Cleveland suburb of Rocky River. It was on a cul-de-sac, nicely located, but with a yard that ended abruptly with a cliff overlooking the Rocky River. Luella was concerned about her two toddlers wandering out of her sight. Cliff was equally concerned and came up with the solution to rig a tethering line to the back yard clothes line. "Tie them to the clothes line?" she wondered aloud. She had no better solution, declaring that Cliff would have to do it. He did. Years later, his two older daughters still kidded him as the Dad who tied them to the back yard clothes line. And he continued to kid them back with the assurance that it was better than tumbling down the cliff into the river. Another source of ongoing family humor was the fact that the only duty assigned Cliff that had much to do with boats and water was several runs on an ice breaker craft that cleared a wintertime channel between Cleveland and Buffalo.

All things considered, Cliff was far more fortunate than many whose duty took them to the South Pacific, some to return blind or otherwise maimed for life, others never to return at all. This did not escape his awareness. At some deeper level the old tug-of-war between his duty to his family and his nation kept churning. And at a deeper level still, his

Navy years turned out to provide a new chapter in the unfolding story of "Cliffie, you're special." as Grandma Dorothea had put it. Being special, he had to learn, included facing up to humiliation and frustration, having to shut up instead of talk, take orders instead of follow his own creative imagination and in general to put with everything that every other sailor in the United States Navy had to put up with. That wasn't all bad, though it took the maturing of time and distance to absorb the lessons he learned while in uniform.

World War II ended with the surrender of the Germans in June and the surrender of the Japanese in early September, 1945. He was discharged in November, to the delight of Luella and the family of two daughters, now a family grown to three daughters with the October arrival of Linda. Getting back into civilian life in the late fall of 1945 went smoothly. WBBM kept his position open and waiting for him. He went back to hosting "Meet The Missus," "Shopping With The Missus" and "Listen To Cliff" during the weekday morning hours. With Luella he had found an apartment in the Hyde Park neighborhood on Chicago's South Side. He was adjusting to his pre-World War II pace without missing a beat.

Like everyone in the Wrigley Building, Cliff Johnson was aware of the commanding presence of Philip K. Wrigley. He was the son of William Wrigley, a high school dropout who was selling soap with the gimmick of giving away a stick of chewing gum with each bar sold, and who went on to build that gimmick into the world-wide corporate giant that Wrigley Gum had become. P.K. Wrigley was a WBBM listener, of course, since its studios were located in the 410 Michigan Avenue building that bore the family name. He had heard Johnson on the air and was an admirer of his speaking and writing skills. Wrigley owned Catalina Island off San Diego, California, and had major business interests, as well as a radio station in California. Something new in that Wrigley-related radio world was in the offing.

The sudden death of Gary Payne, a skilled radio interviewer on KNX, an affiliate station of CBS in Hollywood, had created a vacancy. CBS-Hollywood was beginning the search for a replacement. Word of the opening had reached Chicago. Immediately a group of four accomplished radio veterans were bidding for the California job. Johnson had also learned of the opening. He had heard of it through a friend and advertising man, Arthur Meyerhoff, whose advertising skills had put Krank's Shaving Cream into national prominence. Johnson had known Meyerhoff from his earlier days in Omaha, where on one occasion after hearing Johnson on the radio, he had spoken what seemed like a throwaway line at the time, "…See you in Hollywood sometime." Casual though it was, it still carried a compliment that Cliff Johnson had not forgotten. Meyerhoff was a behind-the-scenes influence on Les Atlas and P.K. Wrigley, with his support for Cliff Johnson as the best choice for the job. When Cliff auditioned and won the position, he had a sense that Meyerhoff, too, had not forgotten the line about seeing him in Hollywood at some future time.

Johnson was a natural for other reasons as well. Cliff and Luella had been invited by Philip and Helen Wrigley as guests in their Lake Geneva home north of Chicago just over the Wisconsin border. The Johnsons had remembered the Wrigley hospitality there, with PK himself serving up soft drinks behind the soda fountain, chatting about his father, the gum business, and the Catalina Island that he loved. Thus a friendship developed that, like many friendships in that context, had a business dimension. Wrigley had quietly put his endorsement to the name of Cliff Johnson in the higher echelon discussions of the right man for the job opening in California.

The basis for a move from Chicago to California was in place. Johnson had, like virtually everyone else in the entertainment world, kept his mind open to Hollywood and the lure of its possibilities. He had loved acting and singing from his earliest school days onward. Why not give Hollywood a try? Furthermore, and even more substantive, was the fact that from 1945 onward, the major Chicago and mid-west radio productions were moving to Hollywood and the tide was irreversible. While many a dream of fame and fortune came crashing down amidst the shallow glamour of Tinsel-Town glitz, the lure was still strong and Cliff felt it. He had a contract for a new job, a new posh location on Catalina Island, and was within a short commute to Hollywood. He was ready to pull up stakes and go.

Luella was not. In 1946, only short months after the family had settled in at the Hyde Park address, she saw no sense in another move so soon after Cliff was settling in with solid promise at WBBM. Above all, she took a dim view of the Catalina and Hollywood scene as a good place to raise their children. But as one who had been trained from her childhood to follow the lead of her husband, she put aside her misgivings and agreed with his decision for the family to move to the west coast.

It was something of an ambiguous portent that Cliff left in February, 1946, with Luella and the girls to follow three months later. His bumpy, twin engine DC3 flight from Chicago to Los Angeles was a nine hour ride, which he braved with high expectations as an aspiring Midwestern folksy radio broadcasting host ready for a crack at Hollywood. While he was obsessed by the ambition to make it behind the microphone, his deeper awareness that his real goal was to preserve a life with a beautiful, devoted wife who was within months of bringing their fourth child into the world. How to keep that driving ambition and the deeper undertow of love for wife and family together was to become the daunting agenda immediately before him.

He checked into the Hollywood Plaza Hotel, the landmark hangout for the in-crowd and movie stars. Arriving with no reservation prompted the desk clerk to arched-eyebrow evaluation as he shakily scribbled his name on the sign-in form. "Is this Mr. Cliff Johnson?" was the somewhat chilly question. "Yes sir," Johnson snapped, and was handed the key. "We have one room left, 503, sir. Elevator to the right." He avoided eye contact with the bell hop, already calculating that the twenty-five dollar per night room was a heavy drain on his final leg of the journey to Catalina Island, the seventy-five acre island some twenty sea miles offshore from Long Beach, California. He quickly forgot the DC3 flight fatigue and made his way straight to Grauman's Chinese Theater, where he walked around the star-shaped symbols embedded in the sidewalk concrete with names he had known since childhood. There was Jimmy Durante with his famous nose imprinted, and John Wayne with his fist. As he went from one famous name to another, he felt the excitement within him rising. Yet his high hopes of landing a big time Hollywood show were tempered by the realistic question if it could ever happen. While it was not entirely out of reach, it was still a long distance away.

In May, Luella and the girls arrived. Cliff had arranged for her to reach Catalina in grand style, securing a pilot friend of his to meet the family at the Los Angeles airport and fly them in a private Cessna to the Catalina airstrip, a somewhat hair-raising landing area that had been hewn out of a rocky ledge of Mt. Blackjack with the Pacific surf directly below. Luella was excited about the arrangements, as excited as an expectant mother with three little ones to watch over can be over a descent in a small plane, through choppy air, over pounding surf, to a narrow strip of runway, newly extended to make it slightly less harrowing. But she and the girls made it. Out of the Cessna they came, with hugs and laughter and happiness all around to be a family united again. Their upscale three bedroom home was one of ten deluxe dwellings in the new Las Casitas section of the Island, with the Chicago Cubs spring training baseball diamond just beyond their back yard. The girls were goggle-eyed at their new surroundings, the birds, the animals, the Catalina flora and fauna, and the vast Pacific beyond. It was exciting for Luella, now that she was there. But it was also a long way from home and her South Dakota roots serving the values and way of life she would not ever fully lay aside. A new chapter in the Johnson family story had begun, in a new setting, amidst new excitements, with new opportunities at hand—and new developments that were to have long range results, well beyond the idyllic Island of Catalina and the Hollywood that was but a half hour flight away.

CHAPTER 4

Get Out Of This Town Before It Devours You

Catalina Island was an idyllic getaway for Hollywood celebrities and other notables seeking refuge from the fast track grind of having to be perpetually charming, chic, and sought after. William Wrigley had turned the Island into a paradise for the privileged few, as well as the annual spring training location for his Chicago Cubs baseball team. The lush baseball complex was within sight of Luella's back yard window. A main feature of the Island was the Wrigley-built Casino which in one respect was unlike any other casino anywhere. Soft drinks only were served at the bar plus its storied menu of chocolate sundaes and other ice cream delicacies. It was not unusual, then, to find people of note discovering that it did not take booze to enjoy amiable conversation, sometimes with the founder of the chewing gum empire himself when he was in residence.

The Casino also hosted such name bands as Benny Goodman, Tommy Dorsey, Les Brown, Harry James, Kay Kaiser and other top bands of the Big Band era. Cliff hosted radio programs from the main ballroom, which required formal attire. Since no cars were allowed on the Island and taxis were rare, Cliff would arrive for work, tuxedo clad, on his bicycle, a sight that did not diminish his image as a man of the people who kept the dress code. It was a minor inconvenience when compared to the sheer delight of living in a corner of paradise just twenty-five miles across a stretch of the Pacific Ocean from Long Beach.

His major program was a radio interview format. Cliff's job was to find ways to book well-known people for interviews without being so intrusive as to be turned down and yet aggressive enough to reach them. These people, many with well-tended egos, were far from the Midwestern housewives who would thrill to a radio star phoning them at home. Yet they were not beyond being surprised and flattered by an approach typical of Johnson's inventiveness. He would scan the hotel registry lists and keep an ear open for local word on famous people arriving, many of them on luxury yachts that would tie up at the local marina after the trip over from Long Beach. Knowing where they might be found, he rented a whaling boat and with megaphone in hand would ease up alongside, boom out the celebrity's name, state his credentials as a CBS radio host, and ask for an interview. Not many, if any, had ever been addressed via a megaphone from a whaling boat. It was sufficiently novel, amusing, and good public relations to be thus approached. And it worked. In fact it worked so well that he soon needed a go-fer to expand the coverage of the rich and famous, who, if pleased to be paged at poolside at the Hollywood Plaza, were equally pleased to have their names announced via megaphone by a CBS radio host pulling up alongside in a whaling boat.

His first interview was with Errol Flynn. In spite of the Flynn's reputation as Hollywood's most notorious womanizer, along with his movie image as the swashbuckling pirate or dashing hero, Johnson found him to be surprisingly gentle and anything but overbearing. He remembered the lesson taught him by Orson Wells some years earlier in Omaha to avoid going for the jugular with opening questions that could titillate or stir controversy. He prepared well for these interviews, getting as much background information on the person as he could. But the dark side was not what he sought, and that was something of a welcome relief to those who were wary of cheap journalism. His method was to begin with an opening inquiry that was benign but not banal and wing it from there. The first response set the tone for the remainder of the fifteen minute interview, often following a famous person such as Errol Flynn on unexpected paths of stories of their family background, off-camera pastimes, and why Catalina was a welcome respite for a time.

Claudette Colbert was another early interview that was timely. She had just finished co-starring with Clark Gable in "It Happened One Night," a film that caught on famously with its motel room scene that reflected the Hayes Office influence of toned-down sexuality. Colbert not only saw to it that Gable stayed in the other bed all night long, but rigged up a bed sheet to provide a modesty curtain that certified their separate sleeping arrangements. When Clark Gable, accepting his side of the curtain, prepared for bed by stripping off his shirt to reveal that he wore no undershirt, the men's undershirt sales across the nation soon took a nose-dive. It was an early indicator of the potency of the movie screen on American culture and customs. Colbert spoke of that and other aspects of her life that she found interesting and worth mentioning in an interview.

The interview with Earl Warren, then the governor of California, was held in the Johnson backyard in a sunlit patio turned into one of the more appealing radio studios anywhere. His response to Johnson's opening inquiry about his family led to conversation about his father, an immigrant boy from Norway of whom Earl Warren was immensely proud. He spoke of the opportunities that were open to his family and to countless other immigrant families who had found an open door to freedom and achievement in America. That, in turn, moved the interview to Warren's passion as an advocate of human rights for all Americans, especially the melting pot people who lacked the connections common to well-established families of prominence and wealth. Johnson remembered that interview when Warren moved on to Washington to join with presidential candidate Thomas Dewey as the vice-presidential candidate in their unsuccessful campaign in 1947. When President Dwight Eisenhower appointed Warren to the Supreme Court as Chief Justice, Cliff and Luella remembered his parting words on their patio to the effect that: "Human rights will always be the wandering torch for the human family's freedom and dignity." They were more than platitudes. The Warren Court handed down the landmark decisions centered in civil rights and the constitutional rights of individuals that ended school segregation in 1954, the one man, one vote rulings, and the guarantee of the right to counsel on the part of those whose charges resulted from police abuse.

Robert Mitchum was among the more memorable interviews on the program, both for the place and the posture of the persons interviewed. The go-fer had succeeded in finding Mitchum at the Atwater Hotel on the Island and steered Johnson to the right room. When he entered he was startled to find the movie tough-guy stretched out flat on the floor on his stomach, engrossed in the manuscript of a play that he was writing with Agnes Moorhead. She was likewise stretched out on the floor opposite him, chin propped in hands, working through the text. Cliff announced himself and his purpose. Mitchum hardly looked up. Yet he responded readily to Johnson's lead-in questions, talking into the microphone which Cliff held down at the floor level in order to be heard. Improbable as the setting was, the interview went on successfully, with the host kneeling down to keep the mike in place so that two very well known Hollywood personalities could keep working on their play while responding to a radio interview at the same time. What caught Johnson most by surprise was Mitchum's eventual comment, offered almost as an afterthought: "Oh yeah, I have a college degree . . . but not a PhD like Agnes!" (who did, in fact, earn her doctorate in the performing arts at a mid-western university). Mitchum talked of his early days… "as a punk of fifteen, a school drop-out, an unhappy kid," who had nevertheless fought his way through formidable barriers to get his college degree. What amazed Mitchum most, he said while finally looking up to make the point with emphasis, was that of all people, he had made it in Hollywood. His manner was a genuine expression of awed humility, the opposite of the expected tough guy, sometimes sullen, often arrogant persona he projected on the screen.

The Mitchum-Moorhead interview had a future beyond the occasion itself, laden both with promise and peril. In Hollywood, Bud Ernst, the CBS producer of two national network programs, "Heart's Desire" and "Queen For A Day" had caught Johnson's interview and liked what he heard. He called Cliff at Las Casitas, the spectacular place where the Johnson's were at home, asking Cliff to come over to Hollywood for an audition as host for both programs. Ernst's image of what was needed was the essence of a shrewd, Hollywood-style sophistication at work—or was it pseudo-sophistication? Johnson represented a kind of mid-western cornball-with-panache. "Cliff, you think, talk, and sound like a mid-westerner. That's what we want on this 'Queen For A Day' program. Pile on the down-home stuff." The audition clicked and Johnson was excited about the step up to national network programming. It supplied the needed lift and confidence that would carry Johnson into the near term future. That meant promise. Furthermore, his Catalina Island program contract was ending and he needed work. Hollywood was calling and he was more than ready to jump at the chance.

There was peril as well. Luella felt it immediately. She was not in any way enthralled by the Hollywood scene. It only underscored her misgivings about the whole California venture and heightened her worries about her husband as a thirty one year old man of talent and obsessive ambition to make it in the fantasy world of the global capitol of glamour. She did not welcome the prospect of his absence throughout the week and weighed the plus of a spectacular career advancement against the odds of the Sunset Boulevard lifestyle of booze, beautiful women and the folly of equating life with celebrity. She saw in the Bud Ernst phone call an invitation to potential disaster, fearing that Hollywood would bring upon her husband the ruin that had done in so many other brightly hopeful aspirants. Her South Dakota roots and instinctive sense for phoniness were intact and, while she accepted Cliff's acceptance of the new job, she did not share his zest for it.

There were other reasons for her misgivings. She was home with three small children and a fourth on the way. Cliff took the Hollywood position and began the commute home for weekends in the autumn of l946. On November 18 of that year, Vicki arrived, bringing the number of Johnson daughters to four. As if to mock her deeply felt dismay, Cliff could not be with her for the birth. Rough Pacific Ocean weather cancelled all passenger service to the Island. It was circumstance not choice that kept Cliff away at a critical time when he desperately wanted to be at Luella's side. The regret he felt laid a burden upon him that he would haunt him ever after. As excited and hopeful as he was about his big break in Hollywood, he could not dismiss the ominous question whether another kind of break might be threatening, one that would erode and finally destroy marriage, family and the deepest values that he had cherished throughout his days.

The "Queen For A Day" program was broadcast from the Earl Carroll Theater in Hollywood before an audience of mostly women between four and five hundred people. It was a format tailor made for Cliff's strongest talents, much like the former programs in Chicago. In interviewing women, the key was getting at who they were and what was interesting about them, and to do in a matter of seconds. Out into the audience Cliff would go, microphone in hand, moving up and down the aisle and choosing participants at random. "How did you meet your husband?" …"Tell me about the best day of your life so far!"…."What's exciting to you at the moment?" were typical openers. When the initial response showed promise, Cliff would lead the woman up onto the stage, continue the interview, and then bring out the crown and red robe for the big moment of being declared *Queen For A Day*. Then followed gifts of a dinner out at a prestige restaurant, a shopping certificate at a premier woman's store, or at the high end, a Caribbean cruise. All this was prelude to a royal escort down the aisle and out of the theater to a waiting limo for a grand tour of Hollywood, including a stop at one of the studios and possibly a glimpse of a famous star or starlet. Sometimes the woman randomly chosen was too frightened to remember her name, and Cliff had the talent to make her feel important anyway, steer around embarrassment, thank her for coming, and move on to the next participant. And sometimes the random choices were memorable. Cliff kept the tape of the interview with the woman who told of her beginnings as a barefoot girl from a sharecropper family in the American South, who fought her way out of poverty to gain an education, a marriage and family and a dignity that outshone the lesser glow of crowns, red robes and limo tours of the town. During the half hour program some three or four women would be crowned, to return home with a lifetime of memories and stories to tell of their brush with royalty, Hollywood style.

Amidst this swirl of rapid ascendancy toward national network radio stardom, Cliff felt the undertow of complications that were continuing to build. The previous show host, Jack Bailey, a man with great radio talent and winsome personality, was slowly sinking into alcoholism. It wasn't called alcoholism in the 1940's; the jargon was "hitting the bottle." Bailey could neither hide nor hold his excessive drinking which had reached the level of a fifth of bourbon daily. Bailey's drinking pal was Bud Ernst, the radio producer who had brought Cliff to Hollywood from Catalina. The first day Johnson was on the job he was introduced to the way of life that revolved around the morning libation. He arrived at the Earl Carroll Theater at 10 a.m., several hours early in order to prepare for the "Queen For A Day" program. Ernst and Bailey greeted him by putting a fifth of Jack Daniels on the table and pulling out the paper cups for the first round of the morning.

Cliff was not prepared for this. While he knew that drinking on the job was common enough in the entertainment industry, he knew he could not enter that world at that level of excess and survive. Soon after that opening shock, word came down from the principal sponsors of the show, including Walter Schwimmer, the advertising representative for Alka Selzer (the program commercial featured an Alka Selzer capsule dropped in a glass of water close to the mike with the signature phrase: "...listen to the fizz"). Schwimmer told Bailey he had to go. Bailey took the decision seriously, telling Johnson that he was "taking a few days off." He meant that he was taking the time out to dry out, unable to deny any longer that booze was not only threatening his career but also his life as well. Schwimmer was not convinced that Bailey could dry out sufficiently to return to the pressures of show hosting. He had to see results first. Moreover, he had Cliff Johnson in the wings to take over the show.

But the decision to drop Bailey troubled Johnson. He truly admired Bailey for his talent and did want to see him lose it all to drinking. Shortly after the decision on Bailey, Johnson heard that Bailey was joining the Alcoholics Anonymous program. He called Bailey's wife to encourage her and the recovery program her husband had entered. It soon appeared that Schwimmer's tough love strategy on Bailey was working. Bailey returned to the program and in so doing gave Johnson reason to demur on his role as partner-host with Bailey. He was learning first hand about the perils that went with fame and success in the Hollywood version of life. Bailey's turnabout from alcoholism earned him a return to hosting the program. He held the position successfully for the next seven years and did not take another drink as long as he lived. That lesson was not lost on Johnson. He would draw upon it sooner than he realized. Moreover, it was satisfying to help an able man find himself and return where he belonged with his exceptional talents. Cliff could take no pleasure as the replacement who won the job at the expense of an admired friend.

As the "Queen For A Day" door of opportunity closed, other doors opened. Not the least of them was a real door to a real house in the San Fernando Valley where Cliff had moved with Luella and the girls. That arrangement, while still not ideal in Luella's mind, was nevertheless a step toward stabilizing the family life that both Cliff and Luella valued immensely. Another door opened, this time a career door of opportunity, as Cliff came into contact with John Guedell, a writer and producer for Art Linkletter's wildly popular "House Party" program. Guedell had known of Johnson through his hosting of "Queen For A Day," and also knew of his work as host of "Money On The Line," another popular radio interview show. Cliff had meanwhile picked up quickly on the importance of having lunch at the Brown Derby Restaurant in Hollywood, the place to see and be seen. Guedell was there often. He saw and heard Johnson on one occasion that was a combination of sheer luck and shrewdness in setting up a typical Hollywood moment.

To be paged at the Brown Derby, to have a phone brought to the booth where one was sitting, was the epitome of Hollywood haute culture. It happened for Cliff. He was paged by name and heard his name boomed throughout the restaurant as the phone was brought to his table. What only Cliff knew was that the person calling was not a major Hollywood producer or a network executive from Chicago or New York. It was an old Navy buddy on the line, calling him as per prior arrangement cooked up by both of them as a ruse to hype the Johnson name.

Guedell was impressed. Conversation ensued. The outcome was a contract for Cliff Johnson to become Art Linkletter's chief backup show host for "House Party" (Johnson framed the contract and has it hanging on the wall of his home to this day). Johnson's assignment was audience warm-up with sure fire jokes, music and banter, until it was time for Linkletter to come onstage and work his magic of the lively art of entertaining conversation with women and children. Cliff did one "House Party" program in Linkletter's place during the time he was under contract. That in itself was a huge boost for his career status, since the Linkletter endorsement was implicit in turning over the show to him when he could not host it himself.

Throughout the time of working with Linkletter, his mind was absorbing the natural genius of children to snag and hold an audience's attention when artfully led to do so. As he took in the whole dynamic of the

"House Party format," he was laying the foundation for a future in similar programming, this time with Luella and his own children. Another important facet of the Linkletter connection was for Johnson to see up close the qualities of an entertainer who had begun life as an orphan in a Canadian orphanage under the auspices of the Baptist Church, and who rose to prominence without losing his soul in the long, hard, upward climb. Linkletter's personal example would become an example of prime importance in the near future. On the surface, things could not have been better for Cliff. What he had worked for from his late teens onward was now a reality. He had made it at the level where it counts, in the entertainment capitol of the world. He had proven himself by experience. He had paid the price of frequent moves, each time upward to another rung on the ladder of career achievement. He had connections that were essential for a flowering career. He loved it, and more than he realized, he was obsessed with the magnetic power of engaging an audience, bringing out what people had inside and doing it for a hefty salary that he could take home to his wife and family who were waiting for him dutifully in "the house in the Valley"—a phrase that symbolized the pinnacle of domestic achievement in Hollywood which was a twenty minute commute away.

But as the lively Brown Derby lunch conversations increased, as well as the cocktails at the lengthening lunch hours, the table at home was increasingly silent. Clifford and Luella Johnson were experiencing the early onset of marital crisis. They had little to talk about at mealtime because their worlds were increasingly divergent. In all likelihood, Luella had talked over her dilemma with Betty Furness with whom she would sometimes sit for Cliff's programs at the Earl Carrol Theater. Furness was a veteran Hollywood actress who knew where the mine fields lay. As the wife of Bud Ernst she had first hand experience in what the dead ends and potholes there were on the Hollywood fast track. Luella had no one else with whom to talk of such things, plus the fact that she grew up in a tradition that favored suffering in silence rather than bearing one's soul on matters of such seriousness. In any case, the mealtime silences at home were growing more ominous. Even with four little girls in the household, the communication was shriveling as this young wife and husband were struggling to reach out to each other without knowing how to cut through to the real issues that were threatening their future.

The bubble burst one evening as supper was ending. Luella looked up from her plate and broke the silence with a quiet ultimatum: " I love you a lot...I'm going home." It stunned Cliff. Yet down deep he could not be altogether surprised. He said nothing in response, but got up and walked in silence around the house, not knowing what to say but feeling a rising panic over the crisis that could be denied no longer. Cliff Johnson was never without words, the right word, the engaging phrase, the lively comment when interviewing thousands of people in times past. But now he was speechless. In this moment, unlike any other in their ten years of marriage, he was without words. The mute condition was surely the culmination of guilt, love for Luella, ambition, devotion to the girls, career obsession, failure, success and at a deeper level the resurgence of the old demons of accusation for not becoming a Lutheran pastor. The haunting questions never went away completely. Did he let his parents and Grandma Dorothea down? Did he fail Luella by denying her deeper wisdom about Hollywood and its toxic potential for poisoning their deepest beliefs and values? Did he offend God by turning his talents to radio instead of religion?

Luella was unshakable in her determination to save the marriage by leaving California. She meant it when she said she loved Cliff and was taking the girls home. It was an act of enormous courage, surely the end result of a long process of waiting, praying, hoping, and finally deciding to do the best thing she could do. She could not help regarding herself as a failure by returning home to her husband's parents without her husband. She could hardly foresee the outcome of her actions, nor could she calculate whether her going home would convince Cliff of what she knew all along, that Hollywood was not success but disaster wrapped in tinsel and hidden behind empty bourbon bottles. She left not because she stopped loving Cliff but because she loved him and the children with a fierceness that would not cave in to the devouring forces she sensed from the first news of the West Coast venture. She saw what Cliff was too immersed in those forces to see. Knowing that Luella was irrevocably resolute, Cliff could only assent to her decision, send her and the children on their way and begin to count the cost of his decision to take on Hollywood and all that went with it.

The train station farewell was tearful. Cliff could sense both warmth and stiffness in Luella's embrace a mixture of love and remorse, of determination and desperation. As the train pulled out he looked down to see a bootie that Linda had dropped while boarding. He held it in his hand as the train gained speed and was gone, a visible symbol of the emptiness that overwhelmed him now that the dearest people in his life were heading home—while he returned to an empty shell of a house no longer a home. Dazed by the sudden sequence of events which Luella's resolute decision had triggered, he found his way back to the house in the Valley and then to Hollywood for a sequence of seventy two hours unlike any he had experienced before.

The next day Cliff hosted his last "Heart's Desire" show. His contract had expired. His dilemma was a mixture of relief and anxiety, relieved that the termination of the show moved him closer to Luella's vision of the future and anxious because he was technically out of a job. The Linkletter/ Guedell contract was there for him with all of its career promise, but that promise collided with the deeper conviction that no career could supplant Luella and the family.

He went from the "Heart's Desire" stage out the door of the Earl Carroll Theater to Billingsley's Restaurant, a small café that was a frequent hangout for show people. In walked Betty Furness, a woman with unusual

savvy about Hollywood and human nature. One look at Cliff's face told
her what she already sensed. She had known Luella and talked with her,
woman to woman. There was an irony about the fact that their husbands
were up to their ears in producing and hosting shows intended to convey
a regal happiness to women listeners. Furness read the irony of the crisis
moment perfectly and got right to the point: "Cliff, get out of this town
before it devours you." That was all and it was enough. Furness was not
offering a suggestion. She was handing down an ultimatum delivered
with that feminine instinctive force that men reject at their peril.

Cliff got up and walked the seven blocks from the Billingsley to the "It
Café." The latter took its name from Clara Bow, the "It Girl" who
embodied the full range of Hollywood glitter in the two-letter pronoun:
It. Not the personal She. Rather, the impersonal It. It signaled a life,
bathed in glamour and surface beauty, that was a commodity, a thing, a
skin-deep lure, a exterior that demanded acceptance with no further
questions asked. It, the "It Café," was the perfect metaphor for the
Hollywood against which Luella rebelled and with which Cliff was
engaged in the battle for his soul and life. The seven blocks were not
lengthy. Yet as Cliff walked them he saw his whole life span flash before
him: Grandma Dorothea's dubbing him special, the farm family years,
the plow seat orations to the corn rows, the first crystal radio set, The
Cadet Quartet tour to Chicago, the college path toward the ministry,
Henkin's prophetic word on talking good, the death of his brother, marrying Luella, the radio career path, Omaha and George and Gracie Allen,
the Twin Cities, then Catalina and now Sunset Boulevard along which he
was almost sleepwalking, trying desperately to sort out life-defining decisions. The confusion in his mind, however, could not surmount the clarity of Betty Furness' words that went from his ears to his heart: "Do it,
Cliff, get out of this town. Do it now before it eats you up."

At the "It Café," once again as if radar-directed, he sat down with his
friend Bud Ernst. Ernst was the type who dealt with serious matters by

humor—really funny, spontaneous stories that become a temporary escape from reality. Ernst announced that he and his drinking buddy, Pat Butrum, well into their cups, had been to Gene Autry's place ("Artery," as Ernst paraphrased) where they had brought in an electric lawn mower and "mowed Artery's carpet." Now it was time to celebrate the success of the prank and Ernst poured the bourbon generously. Cliff was just vulnerable enough to drink it, as if alcohol could tamp down the fires raging in his soul. The stories went on, how Ernst and Butrum had located a giant crane near the Long Beach marina and under cover of night lifted a huge luxury yacht and plunked it down in some celebrity's back yard pool where it would bring sure-fire astonishment the next morning. More stories. More bourbon shots, chased by beer—a combination well below the Sunset Boulevard standards of sophisticated drinking.

By this time Johnson knew he had to get himself back to the Hollywood Plaza Hotel before he would have to be carried back. He made it on his own. In the lobby he saw a sight that stopped him cold. It was Hugo Carlson, the Augustana College speech teacher who had taught Cliff the art of language and the power of speaking words as they were meant to be pronounced. Cliff had helped Carlson get to California to a broader field in drama and radio. Carlson's greeting followed a quick assessment of Cliff's condition: "Hello Farmer, are you all right?" The "Hello Farmer" was a phrase from the past. It had been Carlson's favorite, nickname for Cliff and it carried not ridicule but respectful endearment. Cliff's answer was a terse, "I'm OK." It was one of those necessary lies that both acknowledge and avoid another who means well. This was not the time or place for Johnson to renew an old friendship. But the surprise moment had helped to steady him.

He made his way up to the fifth floor, found his room, but could not stay inside. He went out to pace the hallway, his head in his hands. The elevator doors opened as Cliff stopped opposite them. Again, as though angels were arriving on cue, out stepped Howard Ketting and Charles

Atwater, Wrigley Gum executives from Chicago who were in town on business. They sized up the bourbon-soaked agony of the man outside the elevator door and asked "Can we help you?" When Cliff answered, "This is no place for a South Dakota farm boy." They recognized the voice instantly, having heard Cliff during earlier days at CBS in Chicago's Wrigley Building. The sight of Howard Ketting, whom Cliff knew slightly, brought back immediate recall of Ketting's stories that were fabled for their humorous punch among the Chicago CBS radio people. One memory that came back to him was when Cliff and Fahey Flynn were at lunch in Chicago with Ketting, who had lost an eye earlier in his life. He always carried a spare glass eye and when he got up for an errand in the restaurant, he nonchalantly placed the extra glass eye on the table before Johnson and Flynn, telling it to "keep an eye on these guys till I get back." That background with Johnson was enough to enable Ketting to deliver a straightforward word to Cliff, then and there, in the hotel hallway: "You get out of this place, Cliff." This was the third ultimatum within recent hours, the first from Luella, then from Betty Furness, and now from Howard Ketting. In that order of importance, each came from people who cared enough for Cliff to tell him the truth. He was getting the message, for each one spoke to his best self, his truest priorities, his deepest love—which was of course for Luella and the girls.

He found his hotel room, flopped into bed with his clothes on, and slept off the bourbon, and by morning was in better shape to face what he had to do. It was a Friday now; in June of 1947. He was still in something of a daze as reality settled in on him. He was faced with walking away from a career achievement for which he had given his all for more than ten years. He had arrived. A golden future lay ahead in Hollywood. He had confidence that he could hold his own with the best talent in his field. It was also true, however, that he actually had no firm job. He called John Guedell of the Linkletter connection. When Cliff told him that Luella and the girls had left for South Dakota, Gudell mentioned an opening as host for "Welcome Traveler," another interview radio show. But the tilt of his mind and soul was clearly set toward Luella, the girls, and their future together. He could not and would not put career over those dearest to him.

He was back in his hotel room when the phone rang. It was Les Atlas calling from CBS in Chicago, offering him the position he had left in Chicago a year earlier. The call was like manna from heaven, and it clinched Johnson's decision to pack up and return, first to Luella and the family in South Dakota and then with the family intact back to Chicago. How did the Atlas call come about? What underlay the timing? Cliff never inquired. But his strong hunch was that Ketting and Atlas sent word back to Chicago that the South Dakota farm boy was wise to the fact that Hollywood was not his town. That word had reached Philip Wrigley and Les Atlas. That was the likely route through which the offer came.

Now, fully conscious of what he should do and ready to do it, he geared up to leave Hollywood, clearer than ever that he loved Luella and the family more than career success. He called home to the family in Beresford. His father answered. Cliff told him he was coming home. His father's response was perfect, not a request for chapter and verse on what was going on, but simply… "I'll meet you in Omaha and bring you home!" Then he handed the phone to Luella. "I'm coming home" he began. She repeated his words to make sure she was hearing him correctly, but could get no further before a flood of tears made speech impossible. All the pent up worries, frustrations, hopes, and prayers poured out through her emotions and Cliff was feeling the same. Two days later he was on the train eastward, to home, to Luella, to four little girls excited to hug him, to his parents and family and to the position in Chicago that was his as soon as he arrived.

It was an interesting detail that when Joseph Johnson drove the two hundred miles round trip from Beresford to Omaha to meet Cliff, he brought along an old friend who was a whiz with cars. Ole Wevik was straight out of central casting as a Norwegian-American with a well-earned reputation as the best auto mechanic in Beresford. His nickname was Flunkie, perfect for his modesty of station in life but by no means a term of disrespect. If anyone in or around Beresford needed a car repaired, Flunkie was the go-to guy. It was reassuring for Cliff's father to have a mechanic of Flunkie's quality along for the Omaha trip. Was he also a possible buffer against conversation about the more sensitive side of what Cliff and Luella had been through? The train station meeting of father and son was warm and genuine. The hours of car travel back to Beresford were more silent than spoken between father and son. Flunkie's occasional short sentences punctuated the long silences. "Corn lookin' good." "New silo over there—good shape." "Never seen better roads…" Such were Flunkie's contributions to the welcome, yet awkward, reunion of father and son. It was one of those frequent father-son relationships when much is left unspoken that probably should be spoken, but remains hidden and buried nonetheless, sometimes by circumstance, sometimes by choice. In that time and place, for Cliff and his father it was more circumstance than choice to keep the silence on things that mattered. What was important was to know by whatever means of unspoken communication, that things were OK. A father was deeply glad that his son was back. A son was no less glad and grateful that he wasn't on trial but accepted, loved and comforted by a father who didn't have to say much. As is so often the case in communication among men, much gets said without words. Love is known and felt by the absence of prying, oft-times judgmental asking, or what is worse, mindless chatter that Abe Lincoln must have had in mind when he observed that "it's better to be silent and be thought a fool than to speak and remove all doubt."

The reunion of Cliff and Luella and family was heartfelt, joyous, and purposefully brief. Cliff spent a week at home with the family and then continued on to Chicago to find housing and settle into the work. What awaited him, Luella, and the girls was more than he could hope for. It would be work, good work, that would involve all six of the Johnson family.

The time was at hand when the seeds of a family radio program, germinating for years, could sprout at last. And sprout they did.

CHAPTER 5

Breakfast With The Johnsons

Cliff's re-entry into life and work in Chicago went smoothly overall. But he wasn't too sure about that as he approached the Wrigley Building on his first day back at work in July, 1947. He had to deal with some jitters, being uncertain how he would be received by his friends and former associates at CBS after a year's absence. Before entering he paused at the corner of Michigan and Wacker to collect himself before crossing the bridge over the Chicago River directly in front of the building. He recalled his feelings of nervous anticipation when standing on the same spot six years earlier. As a newcomer to Chicago he was unsure of the Wrigley Building's location and asked a policeman how far it was. "How far can you spit?" was the reply that stuck in his memory and he smiled when recalling it. This time he knew well enough where the Wrigley Building was, though his mouth was too dry to try a repeat of the cop's suggestion. Now it was not where the building was but what awaited him inside that was on his mind.

He entered the building and took the elevator to the second floor. The surroundings were familiar enough; the same receptionist was at her desk. He had good reasons to feel at home. The Chicago papers were already putting a positive spin on his return from the Hollywood venture. He knew he had a secure job. The "Listen To Cliff" morning program was his as soon as he could start up again. He had Les Atlas' personal phone call offer to bank on, and behind that the endorsement of Philip K. Wrigley himself. What he didn't know was what kind of conversation might well be making the rounds behind the scenes among the CBS staff. Did the office gossip peg him as a winner or loser? Why, really, did he come back? And despite the Atlas invitation, where did he really stand with Les Atlas? The linchpin figure of the whole operation had not been happy about Johnson's departure for California over a year ago. His highly popular and profitable "Listen To Cliff" program had to be dropped when there was no more Cliff to conduct it and Atlas was a man with a long memory about station loyalty. Cliff sat down on a reception room chair to collect himself, feeling almost like a visitor in this place that was familiar to him, yet was now new to him. He saw new faces among those passing by, and acknowledged the quick "Hello, glad you're back" greetings from others who remembered him. The re-entry ice wasn't broken, however, until Fahey Flynn saw him, stopped, sat down beside him, spoke as him warmly as an understanding friend, and thus put to rest the nagging misgivings and the case of nerves they brought on. Flynn was already an established fixture in Chicago radio and would become ever more prominent as the 1950's and '60's came and television arrived. He anchored the nightly CBS television news through these decades with unsurpassed ratings based on his reassuring manner and bow-tie signature presence. Even as he conveyed confidence to Cliff in the reception room conversation, he became a kind of psychological anchor for millions of Chicago area viewers trying to make sense of the reportage of turbulent times in the land. Talking with Flynn did it for Johnson. He was really back with no reason to second guess the reception he would receive.

He resumed hosting "Listen To Cliff" the next day and felt the old confidence surging back during his first week on the job. But he had not yet talked to Les Atlas. The anticipation of that meeting did give him pause and made him wait for a week, still not knowing what he would hear from the top man at CBS Chicago. On the first day of his second week of work the time was right. He approached Atlas' door and lightly tapped before entering. From inside he heard a "yes" and moved tentatively into the office. "Skipper? Johnson asked, using the only title that anyone ever used when addressing Les Atlas. Johnson's voice told Atlas who it was that entered. He was seated in his swivel chair, facing the window with his back to the entrance door, his head tilted downward, his eyes on the Wall Street Journal, not looking up. It was a vintage Les Atlas moment, neither rude nor effusive but monosyllabic in his response. When Johnson began to speak, wisely choosing not the California experience now past but a program idea for the future, Atlas turned to face him as he listened. Cliff moved right into his vision of a half-hour program with children, his own children and Luella, in a "Breakfast With The Johnson's" format that would originate from the family kitchen table before the kids were off to school. It was a distillation of the ideas that had begun in the CBS studio several years earlier when the eighteen-month-old Sandy had piped up with her on-air request to go to the bathroom. The idea had grown as he watched and worked with Art Linkletter in interviewing children in Hollywood.

Atlas heard him out, gave the idea a moment's thought and responded with four words: "Wire it up tomorrow." That immediate affirmation got the Johnson adrenaline flowing full force, as he experienced one more expression of that unerring Atlas instinct for an idea with a future. With the critical endorsement and orders to "wire it up tomorrow" in hand, Cliff went to the studio engineers to start the preparations. Their response was predictable, wiring up for a broadcast with small children around a family breakfast table in a Chicago suburb was reason to roll their eyes and wonder aloud, "There goes Cliff again, coming off the wall!" The address for wiring it up was 605 Woodbine in Oak Park, a house that Cliff had learned was for rent through a tip from his CBS colleague, John Harrington.

Studio engineer Bill Ketelhut directed the wiring up project in the Oak Park house, seeing to it that the necessary holes were drilled through the foundation for the wires leading upstairs. Ketelhut set up his equipment in the pantry room just off the kitchen. The next morning the four Johnson girls were up early, still in their pajamas as Luella gathered them around the table. Sandra (7), Pamela (5), Linda (4) and Vickie (2) were unaware of how important that first morning was. The taped audition would be reviewed by the CBS staff to determine whether the program was a go or a no. For the kids it was simply a regular breakfast with a strange man in the pantry who wore earphones and had odd-looking things around him in the pantry. Three microphones were placed on the breakfast table. The girls played like they were sugar bowls.

The mikes went on. The girls, Luella, and Cliff did what they did each morning before breakfast, praying the family prayer of thanksgiving:"God is great, God is good, and we thank Him for our food. Amen." Next came the commercial advertising Nelson Brothers Furniture Company. Cliff touted the quality items and great bargains of the store, ending with the tag line—"Nelson Brothers! From the pictures on the wall to the rugs on the floor, we've got it all!" The ad line portrayed enough of a visual picture to stir up lively response from the girls, especially Sandy and Pamela who started arguing about how all those people in the store could keep track of…and then Sandy inadvertently reversed the commercial words with… "all those pictures on the floor and rugs on the wall." That led to a full two minute back-and-forth between the two girls on where the pictures and rugs belonged. The kids' magic was instantaneous. It was the "pictures on the floor and rugs on the wall" line that was a keeper, and the two minute spontaneous argument that kept the spotlight on Nelson Brothers furniture was unexpectedly effective advertising. The audition tape got the green light at the next day's staff review. "Breakfast With The Johnsons" was on its way for a ten year run that would make the family a household name throughout the twelve state area initially and later nationwide. The date was September 15, 1947.

That Monday morning was unforgettable for Luella. Cliff was a pro before the microphone, but she was petrified, never having set foot in a broadcasting studio, let alone speaking into a microphone. She had two weeks to worry about her radio debut, since Cliff had welcomed her and the girls at the Chicago train station when they arrived from South Dakota. His excited disclosure that "we'll be on the air" made her wonder about the "we." She had visions of lines read from a program script, rehearsals, mikes, studio equipment, 7:30 till 8 a.m. broadcast time each weekday morning, and wondered how she and four young children could ever fit into such a picture. Nothing of the sort, Cliff counseled. The whole program will be informal, no script, no rehearsal, no studio formalities. Cliff explained that the whole family will talk as the Johnson's always talk around the table in their own kitchen, informally, spontaneously, and wide open to any subject that pops up. Luella was hardly convinced by Cliff's buoyancy. She later noted in her diary, "I am afraid that my only contributions would be four magic words: 'Have some coffee, dear.'" True to her worrisome vision of what her role in that first broadcast would be, she poured more coffee and more coffee that morning, finally emptying what little was left into the sink, unable to drink another drop.

Some predicted a short life for the program, but neither Cliff nor Luella let the doomsayers dampen their enthusiastic plunge into an altogether new venture in network radio. While children had been on programs before, no single family of children had entered the high-risk field of public entertainment. But "Breakfast With The Johnson's" caught on early and held its own toward steady growth.

From the start, Luella and Cliff had concerns about how the popularity of the program might spoil their children by giving them airs of superiority over their neighborhood and school friends. It was a well placed concern, given the rapid rise of the program in and beyond the Chicago listening area. It wasn't long before Sandy, the oldest daughter, came home with the comment that one of her girl friends and her teacher spoke of hearing them on the radio. Luella and Cliff took the comment as a challenge to get ahead of the serious problem that a celebrity self-image would surely impose on each Johnson youngster. They took a creative step early on by having special Saturday morning broadcasts for a series of weeks that featured each class of the school where the girls attended. Something as new and exciting as being interviewed on the radio was an instant hit with the children, well worth sacrificing a bit of Saturday morning time for an experience that each would long remember. It had the intended effect of spreading around the fun and fame of being on the radio, and helped blunt the thing that Luella had mightily resisted from the outset, that her children would take on airs of superiority as junior celebrities. The effect was surely positive on Oak Park as a community. It had long been well known as the home of Frank Lloyd Wright and Ernest Hemingway; now it was gaining new attention as the community from which that breakfast program family originated.

It also helped to connect the Johnsons to a church affiliation that would continue long into the future. Otto Geiseman, the pastor of Grace Lutheran Church in nearby River Forest, was among the early circle of listeners. He dispatched his assistant, Pastor James Manz to make a call on the family and invite them to worship at Grace. Since Cliff and Luella both came from strong Lutheran backgrounds, it was natural for them to respond with appreciation for the kind of pastoral leadership that Geiseman offered as well as the Sunday School opportunities for the children. The first row under the pulpit soon became the pew neighborhood regularly occupied by the six Johnsons after they joined Grace Lutheran in October, 1947. On various occasions thereafter Cliff invited Pastor Geiseman to take his place around the breakfast table and enter into whatever subject turned up that morning. Especially for Cliff, this was the first pastoral relationship with depth that enabled him to share some of his deeper experiences carried over from his own early days of unfulfilled aspirations to the pastoral ministry, as well as the baggage brought along from the Hollywood ups and downs. In the early 1950's when Martin E. Marty became the two year assistant pastor under Geiseman, another lifelong pastoral association was established with Luella and Cliff. One of Marty's first publications was a thirty page booklet telling highlights of the Johnson family story; in later years Luella booked all of Marty's air travels to thousands of destinations on his demanding lecture circuit.

By 1949 the 605 Woodbine address was too small for the equipment needed for the daily broadcasts plus the growing needs for room for the growing children. The family had a lot of time together under the same roof. Cliff began to look around for a larger place. He spotted a gem that caught his eye—a big, rambling house on Kenilworth Avenue, which Luella immediately declared out of reach of the family budget. Cliff persisted, however. After driving Luella past the house and not taking issue with her initial objections, he managed another drive-by with her in the car a few days later. He had worked up the case for all the ways he could fix up the rooms for the children and make space for the daily broadcast at home and make an office for himself in the basement. That convinced her, for she knew Cliff did have uncommon fix-it skills inherited from his boyhood days on the farm. They bought the magnificent old Victorian home with room for all seven Johnsons to fit their family and work needs, plus a spare bedroom for family and friends. Cliff located a used billiard table to fulfill a lifelong dream to have one in his home, and Luella had her spacious utility room for attending to her myriad duties as mother, wife, program hostess (and on one occasion hosting it herself for a sick husband) and correspondent with the increasing numbers of listeners writing letters about what they were hearing.

Two complications arose not long after the program had become a permanent fixture on the CBS network's span across a ten state area. The first concerned the table prayers, Scripture, and occasionally a hymn included in the program. Within weeks of the first airing, some murmerings surfaced among a number of CBS staff people about prayer over the airways that belonged to the public. The phrase for the questioning was "It's unusual," with clearly negative connotations. But no one really knew what to do about it. The WBBM sales manager, Ernie Shomo, came to Cliff with the problem and suggested that it might be best to leave out praying or at least to try a few programs without it to see what happens. Cliff was bothered that they were bothered. He took a dim view of dropping something natural to the family morning ritual that flowed seamlessly into the radio broadcast format. But he knew he had to deal with the problem. He went to his pastor, Otto Geiseman, and received sage advice. Geiseman said to drop the prayers but then wait long enough to learn what the audience response would be. His hunch that the demand to return family prayers to the broadcast would be swift and strong. That's what happened. After several programs which dropped the Scripture and prayers, an avalanche of letters and calls poured in, putting an end to any staff questions thereafter. It was a significant commentary on the times. In the late 1940's omitted prayer became included prayer by popular demand. As later decades brought great cultural and religious change, that response would not be likely.

The other complication was of longer duration and had unexpected consequences. Cliff found himself confronted by what eventually resulted in a move from CBS-WBBM Chicago to WGN and the Mutual Broadcasting System. That prospect was because of a challenge raised by AFTRA, shorthand for the Association of Federated Television and Radio Artists, or in shorter hand—the union. AFTRA was part of the AFL-CIO labor establishment. Ray Jones, head of the Chicago area AFTRA, called Johnson in August, 1951, questioning whether the Johnson children were union members. Of course they were not. The idea had never occurred to their parents or to the broadcast people that they should be. But the issue could not be ignored since the whole range of children's voices on the air, from a baby crying to a teenager speaking, was serious union business. The question about the status of the Johnson children originated by an inquiry from Fanny Brice, the famous impersonator of the Baby Snooks radio personality widely known all over America in radio and film. Again, Ernie Shomo of the WBBM staff became part of the conversation on how to respond. He proposed that the two older Johnson daughters, Sandy and Pam, should be on the air two days of the week, with the other younger children off the air, and then alternate the arrangement on the three other days of the week, thus hoping to duck the union issue of children employed on the air full-time. Cliff knew that this made no sense. His children could not talk or be quiet around the breakfast table depending on the day of the week. The problem would not go away. Les Atlas had heard about it, but wanted no part of the union intrusion and waved Cliff off to find his own solution. It became clear to Cliff that he needed topnotch professional and legal help to find the best answer.

He turned to John Moser, a WBBM attorney who was not only a respected lawyer but a friend much valued by Cliff and Luella. He had graduated first in his Northwestern University Law School class and was, in Johnson's view, a man with a keen mind, goodhearted, and notably ecumenical. He had married June Kraft, daughter of John Kraft of the Kraft Food fortune and the two were warmly genuine people who handled their wealth wisely and never lost their charisma for the common touch among people of all walks of life. Moser's own quip in describing his marriage was a union of a 5' 5" Jew with a 5' 4" Baptist, both of whom became Roman Catholics, who lived happily in a bungalow in the Chicago suburb of Morton Grove. Moser rose even higher in Cliff and Luella's esteem after his wife died in her 40's, leaving him to raise their five children as a devoted father. From time to time Moser would call with an invitation to come over for some Jewish penicillin, their term for chicken soup.

Moser's solution was to face the inevitable and bring the entire family in under the AFTRA umbrella. But CBS was adamant against introducing any union nose into its corporate tent and said nothing doing. Moser was realistic about that as well and cared enough about the genius of the program to look around elsewhere for a network home. He was alert enough to learn that WGN of the Mutual Broadcasting System was not only more flexible on the union issue but eager to take on "Breakfast With The Johnsons." He also knew that WGN was the anchor station of the entire Mutual Broadcasting System nationwide, and would mean an exponential jump in stations carrying the program. A promising key to the prospect of a move to WGN was the station owner, the newspaper baron Colonel Robert McCormick who owned the Chicago Tribune and micro-managed its editorial policy and general tone to his distinctive conservatism in political and social matters. But he was an enthusiastic fan of the program and welcomed the prospect of receiving it into the WGN family and thus into the wider MBS network system. Moser negotiated the contract. The Johnson program moved from WBBM to WGN in April, 1951, ending a five-year affiliation and beginning a new radio network home that would continue until 1957. The move propelled "Breakfast With The Johnsons" from a ten state, primarily Midwestern area, to coast to coast coverage served by 154 stations, including such major metropolitan centers as New York City, Cleveland, and Detroit.

Along with Colonel McCormick's enthusiasm for the program (it was his idea to move from a half hour to forty five minutes), another important element in bringing about the change of networks was the support of major corporate sponsors. Moser made sure that George Geyer of Nabisco, John McLaughlin of Kraft Foods, and particularly Leonard Japp of Jay's Potato Chips were firmly on board in promoting the new affiliation and actively supportive in assuring ongoing financial support for the move which would put the Johnson family into millions more American homes at half-past-seven each weekday morning. That statistic had personal meaning for the Johnsons in the form of increased fan mail that came in from all parts of the nation, reaching a volume of two thousand letters per month by the mid-1950's. It was the unrehearsed conversations of the children that triggered the bulk of the letters, with people often asking for answers to their own children and family problems. No subject was taboo on the program; the girls would tee off on themes as diverse as war, clothes, school, divorce, politics, music and one of the more thorny problems emerging in Oak Park and beyond—racial bigotry. One morning in 1951 Sandra broke into the typical small talk on the program and said: "Daddy, my friend, Percy Julian—you met him at my birthday party—told me that their house was set on fire two times. The fire was terrible! He wasn't hurt, though. They don't know who did it. Isn't that bad? Why would someone want to burn their house down?" Cliff chose his words carefully, knowing the subject was volatile, especially as it concerned the Oak Park family of Dr. Percy Julian, a world renowned scientist whose laboratory efforts were yielding many new basic creative medical wonders. "Are the children talking about it?" he asked. Sandra: "Well, yeah, but they don't know much about it, but the teachers and the janitor know. My friend heard them talking in the hall, saying that the Julians are Negroes and Oak Park doesn't want them here." Cliff: "That's is not true, for there were hundreds protesting the burning at the Village Hall in Oak Park yesterday. It wasn't somebody from Oak Park who set the fire. The Julian family will survive. The community, as time passes, come to accept them as important members who do belong here. So, let's pray today for the strength and courage that the Julians and all of us need and for those misguided people who set the fires." Johnson went to Pastor Geiseman for further counsel in the matter, and invited him to be on the program the next morning. Geiseman's contribution was typically straightforward as he spoke to a host of listeners who were not all sure they wanted to hear what a Lutheran pastor had to say about racial bigotry. Geiseman: "There are some people out there who are blind to the truth that God has created people of all different colors, eyes, hair and features. These people who do bad things like setting fire to Dr. Percy Julian's home have developed a dislike, really a hatred, because they are victims of false beliefs which make them think that they are superior to people of color. It might seem hard for you to understand it, but we need to pray, not only for the Julian family but also for those bad people who set fire to the Julian house." It was the advice that conformed directly to what the Johnsons were doing and would continue to do.

There were the lighter moments when the children's candor about sponsor products set Cliff's teeth on edge, but with surprisingly positive results. One of the sponsors was Nabisco which featured Milk Bone Dog Biscuits. The Johnson dog, Echo, was the prime promoter, of course. During one broadcast Vicki reported that Echo was not eating her milk bone, but now loves it. Cliff was glad to hear it, and chimed in with the advertising plug that Nabisco Milk Bone provides great nourishment for all pups. Vicki came back with the comment that Echo wasn't so fond of her Nabisco until she put a dab of chocolate on it. "That's when she really ate it!" Cliff paused long enough to think quickly: "…That makes it a dessert, too" and hurried to another subject. The positive listener response was reassuring that Nabisco stayed on board. In fact their advertising people capitalized on Vicki's comment as a positive product identification line. Vicki had another moment of candor turned in a positive direction. Rohrig Pharmaceutical Products, the producer of ammoniated toothpaste was another sponsor. Vicki, age three, was chosen as the Amion Girl. The company's advertising agency developed a script featuring Vicki literally singing the praises of Amion Toothpaste with an advertising ditty that Vicki spent hours practicing, aided by the national sales manager of Rohrig Pharmacies who came to the Johnson house to set it up. The broadcast moment arrived and Cliff sailed right into it: "Well Vicki, you've been chosen as the Amion Girl. We have it in our bathroom cabinets. Amion Toothpaste is the new way for fighting cavities, great for kids and it's now our family choice. So, Vicki, want to sing the little Amion song now?" Vicki deadpanned: "Daddy, I'm not so sure I like it. I'm still using Colgate's." Cliff gulped and took a minute to backpedal: "Well," with a chuckle to buy a little time, Cliff made the best of it: "Well, four out of five of us use it!" The next few hours were not comfortable for Cliff and for the Rohrig people, wondering what would happened. What happened was a lit-up switchboard with calls to Rohrig and the station from listeners who were delighted with Vicki's honest goof. It made the Chicago Tribune columns and a brief comment in the trades section. Amion reported a 20% boost in sales, thanks to Vicki's being Vicki.

The neighborhood-friendly feel the program conveyed included the regular, rhythmic knock each morning at 7:45 sharp when Bill the milk deliveryman brought in the morning's supply. His noisy "Good Morning, Good Morning" was heard by hundreds of thousands day-by-day, along with his enthusiastic pitch for specials on cottage cheese, butter and a rundown on life from the window of the milk truck. Cliff would needle him from time to time about all the free plugs Bowman Dairy was getting, but never a freebie in return. Bill promised, however, that on his last day before retiring from a thirty five year run, he would load up the Johnsons with freebies galore. And he did. He was the star of the program that final day, and when the Chicago Tribune carried his obituary notice years later, it was headlined "Oak Park Milkman Radio Star Dies." Family pets made the program. When Olaf the parakeet died, after five years as the unofficial treasurer of the family and Luella's special friend, a full program was devoted to the subject of how a family deals with the loss of a pet. One of the biggest mail responses ever came when the program engineer wired a mike to a robin's nest under the garage eave, which enabled a two-week build-up to the first cracking through of the new born chicks. When the Oak Park Fire Department voluntarily sent over a hook-and-ladder truck to help maneuver a new king-size mattress through a second floor porch door entrance (the chief was a regular listener and occasionally appeared on the show with fire prevention tips) it was an event that inspired a story in the town newspaper. Only one letter came back complaining about this use of taxpayer's money, but she made no further fuss, asking only that the Johnsons "sleep on it."

When the four Johnson girls were told that a new family member was on the way, it was inevitable that the subject of where babies came from would arise. The nine-year-old Pamela asked the question with typical directness: "Mom, who put the baby under your heart?" She could see from her mother's swelling middle that there was, indeed, a baby growing inside under the heart. Luella's answer came after a reflective pause: "God put the seed under my heart and it grew," a response that came without difficulty. Other questions calling for clear answers to complex life questions did not come so readily. Luella would often draw from the wisdom she received in the volume of letters and comments that were prompted by on-air Johnson family conversations. Answering letters, particularly those addressed to her, became a major demand on Luella's time.

As February, 1952, approached and Luella's time for delivery drew near, plans were made to continue the regular broadcast from the maternity ward of West Suburban Hospital in Oak Park. Already a month before the baby was born, the lines were installed into the basement area of the hospital that was being prepared as a makeshift studio to herald the new arrival. On February 19th the girls had a baby brother as Clifford T. Jr. made his appearance. After four girls the assumption was that the fifth would be a girl as well. A boy's name had not even been under consideration. When the nurse told Cliff that it was a boy, he asked immediately "How much does she weigh?" He was baptized Clifford Tilman Johnson, Jr., and from early on was given the grown-up nickname "C.T." by the girls and family.

In April of that year another innovation occurred as the Johnsons planned a full dress visit to New York City. Preparations were extensive for they included things necessary for a three-month-old baby. Also required was the recording of at least four program tapes before leaving and four more tapes recorded while in New York which were sent back to the Chicago studio. The Johnsons were booked into the Savoy-Plaza Hotel on Fifth Avenue, courtesy of the program sponsors, and the kids were immediately into the subject of their New York surroundings. Linda came up with a pertinent observation on hotel breakfasts when she saw the bill: "Gee, it's expensive to live in New York! I almost can't swallow all this expensive food—it chokes me." Unwittingly she spoke for the family. Among the exciting activities during the hours following the morning taping was a visit to Warners Theater and a conversation with two premier American comedians, Bud Abbott and Lou Costello. The oldest child, Sandy, was aware of their fame and was intrigued by the antics of Abbott, while the disinterested younger ones stood gawking at everyone else around them.

When business appointments required Cliff and Luella to be out of the hotel briefly, the children stayed in the hotel suite accompanied by a baby sitter. When the parents returned to the hotel and approached their room, they were startled to see the manager and hotel detective on hand and visibly excited. What happened, as they soon learned, was that Pamela, Linda and Vicki had been playing *Cops and Robbers*. Pam had been sitting by an open window and written a note addressed to "Cops" and floated it out the window down onto Fifth Avenue. A pedestrian had grabbed it as it descended in the wind, read it and hurried inside to the manager's office. The note to the cops read "Help in 804!" Help was quick to come, causing the Johnsons to apologize and wonder if they would ever be allowed to return.

The New York visit spanned the Easter weekend which meant the Easter Parade was on the schedule. Luella had been invited to participate and given a magnificent, French-imported hat for the occasion. The hotel public relations director let it be known that it was a two hundred dollar hat, the only one of its kind in New York, and it was irreplaceable. The treasure was stored on a top shelf of a closet, well out of reach of the children who were on notice not to touch it. All went well at the parade which featured Mike Wallace as the Master of Ceremonies. Afterward the family was seated around a big table during the luncheon, and Vicki spoke up to the lady next to hear, commenting on her lovely mink coat, adding that her mother would look equally nice in the mink "…but we really can't afford it." Vicki took the well-groomed lady's pleasant smile as incentive to continue the conversation, announcing with a hopeful tone "…But my mother has a $200 hat she's wearing." Before the impromptu conversation partner could comment on that state of affairs, Vicki confessed the way it was, sadly: "But we can't even afford to pay for the hat, so she has to return it." Luella, beyond Vicki's reach to quash the comments, smiled weakly.

In June, 1951, the Johnsons enjoyed a special event in Cliff's home town of Beresford, South Dakota. It was "Cliff Johnson Day," complete with a gala parade, bands and a special program broadcast from the master control truck set up by the engineer from the MBS network. Governor Sigurd Anderson was present as over a thousand people gathered in the town park for the ceremonies. The governor's message was a tribute to the sound values evident in the Johnson family tradition, made all the more enjoyable as Cliff's mother and father were there take it all in. In his speech of reminiscence of his Beresford beginnings and thanks for the Cliff Johnson Day with all the trimmings, Cliff ended with this comment: "We aren't a glamour family. There are more important things to live for besides a glamour bubble." More than many could realize, Cliff was talking about the more recent past and lessons learned from it. Earlier, President I.D. Weeks of the University of South Dakota had conferred an honorary degree upon Cliff and named him a *Doctor of Ad Liberatum*. When Cliff asked his nine-year-old Pamela if she knew what that meant she thought for a moment and said "It means doctor of baloney, doesn't it, Dad." Among the salutatory greetings read from the podium were telegrams from the South Dakota U.S. senators Karl Mundt and Francis Case, as well as from President Dwight Eisenhower. A closing touch to the South Dakota trip proved to be more than a child's impromptu question to a state official. Out of the blue Pamela had asked Governor Anderson why he didn't have any children. His answer was to the point: "Because the Lord didn't give us any." Her answer was equally to the point, as she saw the matter: "Don't worry, you aren't dead yet." A year or more later the Johnsons were among those who received the good news from the South Dakota governor's mansion announcing the birth of a healthy daughter, Karen.

The Johnsons had developed a way to handle family vacations as the children grew, and vacations were always a family affair with all the children along. The logistics were formidable: packing for five youngsters, two adults, a sound engineer, a secretary called for three cars to handle family and staff plus baggage. At the vacation destination five mobile homes would be waiting to provide housing during the vacation stay. All this provided valuable experience when a two month tour of Europe occurred in the summer of 1955.

It was billed "Operation Home Town America," a broadcast and film tour of England, Norway, Sweden, Germany, Austria, Switzerland, Italy and France. The idea fit in with the post-World War II Eisenhower era of wanting to normalize the people to people relations that had been skewed or severed altogether during the war. It was a concept that had been percolating in Cliff's imagination for years. Now that tourism was reviving and bridges of friendship and understanding were ripe for rebuilding, 1955 struck him as the right time to connect home town America, in this case Oak Park, Illinois, with people of the towns and cities of the eight countries to be visited. The unique feature in it was the continuity of the daily broadcast, now from breakfast tables all across western Europe, Scandinavia and the British Isles, plus on the street interviews and special receptions with people from all walks of life. Now the Johnsons sought to provide a window through which the millions of fans of "Breakfast With The Johnsons" could experience vicariously what most of them could not experience personally, a person-to-person feel for people, common everyday folks, in other places, cultures and languages.

It was a huge task that required knowledgeable planning of the daily itinerary, where to stay, what to eat and how to get from one place to the other for the daily broadcasts that had to be sent home for airing. Cliff called the British Tourism Office in New York and laid out the "Operation Hometown America" concept, which was well received. Further exploration with that agency paid off handsomely. They contacted tourism offices of the other countries on the tour and laid out the daily hotel, meals and transportation arrangements for the six weeks. Another bonus development was the inclusion of Patricia McDermott as public relations director for the tour. She was an experienced European traveler herself, and her contacts with radio, press and government people were invaluable all the way. Cliff hired Roy Cone as his chief engineer for the daily broadcasts, bringing to nine the number in the traveling party.

For financial backing, Cliff turned to two Oak Park business leaders who recognized the promise of the trip, both for the image of Oak Park across the Atlantic as well as the commercial value of daily commercials that reminded listeners who was helping to foot the bill. Harry Bromfield of Lytton's Clothiers, Jon Domeier of Oak Park Federal Savings (an avid traveler himself) and William Gilmore of the local department store came up with a $5000 total as the initial backing. Cliff tapped the U.S. Government funding for Eisenhower's "People-To-People" Program for the second $5000. He put up the third $5000 himself to complete what was necessary.

On June 24th the trip began from New York aboard the S.S. United States for the five-day voyage across the Atlantic to Southampton, and then the rail trip to London. The red carpet treatment began with a visit to the chambers of the Mayor of London for a welcome and then settling in at the Flemming Hotel and setting up for the daily broadcasts in unusually posh surroundings. Following London came ten days in Norway with generous press coverage in a language Cliff could understand and speak from his growing-up days. In Copenhagen they were booked to interview Hans Christian Hansen, the Prime Minister of

Denmark who had sent them an invitation to join him and his family for dinner at the Prime Minister's residence. Luella, who would string up clotheslines in hotel bathrooms all across Europe to keep the family properly laundered, promptly got out her iron and pressed four dress-up outfits for the girls and made sure that she and Cliff were properly attired for the occasion despite the uncomfortably hot weather in Copenhagen at the time. Upon arrival at the suburban manse they were graciously escorted to the backyard where they were greeted by the Prime Minister of Denmark dressed in blue dungaree Levis and a bright yellow sports shirt. Mrs. Hansen politely suggested that the Johnsons loosen up, which happened immediately as the kids shed their fancy tops, kicked off their shoes, removed their socks and all enjoyed a backyard cheeseburger feast. They could not forget Prime Minister Hansen barking out "rare, medium or well done." Cliff and family chimed in with "the works" and the stage was set for a lively interview in which Hansen spoke of his boyhood and family during the war years, how he met Inge his wife, his love for politics and other topics well suited to the person-to-person goals of "Operation Hometown America." In Cologne, Germany, an interview was set up for Konrad Adenauer, the first chancellor of the new Germany and Johnson was eager for the views of this symbolic man of a new era following the disaster of the Hitler years. A last minute intervention of a matter of state prevented his coming. As a courtesy to Johnson he sent his son, Dietrich. Cliff shifted gears quickly as the situation required, devoting the interview recorded in the Gothic magnificence of the Cologne Cathedral to stories of what it was like to grow up as a son in a family that felt destiny's burden imposed upon their father by the post-World War II years.

It was a different atmosphere in Vienna as the city was still under the tripartite governance of American, Russian and British forces. Their hotel was in the Russian sector, which became evident as soon as the family moved into their rooms with the hammer and sickle symbols on the walls. Cliff sensed suspicion and hostility in the air, and was not comfortable with the hotel setting, an impression that deepened with a whispered comment from a French hotel guest about the Russians: "They follow us." Later, Cliff learned that the rooms had been bugged, which made those broadcasts the most stilted and impersonal of the European experience. There were anxious moments of a different sort in Switzerland as they drove through the Brenner Pass in the Swiss Alps. The British-made cars they had rented kept suffering vapor lock in the higher altitudes, requiring unscheduled stops and dousing the carburetor with cold water and making them wish for Flunkie's expertise from back in Beresford. One such stop was on a narrow stretch of the Brenner Pass road. Cliff stopped to look for water and the car emptied, except for Cliff Jr. and Vickie in the back seat. The emergency brake had not been firmly set, and as Cliff turned away to look for water, the car began to roll toward the edge of the precipice. Both he and Patricia McDermott lunged to open the doors on either side and dive for the emergency brake, thus saving the children from what would surely have been a fatal drop down hundreds of feet to the rocks below. Shaken, they settled their nerves, solved the stall problem and drove on toward Berne. In the hotel there, the ingenuity of the children to solve language problems proved itself once again. Sandy and Pam were at breakfast before the rest of the family and wanted some eggs with bacon. When words didn't work with the waiter, they did what kids have no hesitancy to do—mimic the sounds and actions of a chicken and pig. With elbows flapping and clucking noises, plus the universally recognizable grunt of a pig they communicated. The parents arrived to find both girls beaming over their plate of bacon and eggs.

In Paris an unusual connection occurred with a former "Breakfast With The Johnsons" listener. Vito Suciccio grew up with the Johnson morning program in his teenage days in Kenosha, Wisconsin. Later he had been stationed in France with a U.S. Army unit in which he had worked as reed instrument repairman for the famed American band leader, Glenn Miller, also a serviceman assigned to troop entertainment overseas. He stayed on in Europe after Miller's untimely death in his military plane crash and had risen to the presidency of the U.S.A. franchise of the LeBlanc Music Instrument, Inc., the makers of high quality clarinets. Hearing of the Johnson family entourage's arrival at the Cambon Pension Hotel in Paris, he not only found them there but secured four top flight wind instrumentalists to join him in performing a classical musicale to the delight of the Johnsons, hotel guests and passers by. It was one of the more unique person-to-person moments of the six week tour, connecting the Johnsons with a Kenosha, Wisconsin fan from years back with Parisian hotel guests and staff. The memory of it came back years later when Cliff happened upon the obituary notice of Vito Spuciccio whose death at age 81 was noted in a Chicago paper.

The final event of the tour took place the day after the hotel lobby concert, and it was fortunate for the whole purpose of the tour that it took place at the end of the trip. The strain of the non-stop pace for six weeks, the pressure of all the travel, all the interviews, all the daily tapings for broadcast both in Chicago and Europe finally got to Cliff. He collapsed in a faint of exhaustion on a sidewalk near the hotel. He was helped back to the room and slept straight through for twenty four hours, enough to revive him for the trip to board the S.S. United States at LeHavre and the voyage home to New York and then to Chicago. Despite the toll of exhaustion that caught up with Cliff on the last day, the tour had been a resounding success. They had not missed a day of recording for the continuity of the network program back home—the tapes were sent air mail express for the Chicago broadcast just two days after the taping in each European city. Some 7000 feet of film was shot along the way, provided footage for movie programs in churches, schools, clubs and civic groups around the midwest. Luella had kept Cliff and the five children scrubbed, laundered, pressed and well dressed throughout the daily demands of well-publicized appearances. Oak Park had become more than a name on the map to many abroad, and the adage that everybody loves kids was proven across foreign boundaries. Prominent people from the international world criss-crossed the Atlantic often. It was unique that a family of seven made the journey, building bridges by being themselves, burnishing a more positive image of Americans overseas and broadening horizons at home.

On the day after their late August return to Oak Park, the town turned out for a Welcome Home Parade down Oak Park's main avenue. Tired but happy, the Johnsons enjoyed a red carpet celebration, with WGN favorite (and Chicago Cubs baseball announcer) Jack Brickhouse handling the master of ceremony honors. The town had received a wider window on the world and the daily breakfast broadcast took on new dimensions of international commentaries on what a family learns by listening and talking to people along the way. Amidst all the hoopla, fun and demanding work of the tour, however, an awareness was growing in the back of Cliff's mind. The children were growing up. Radio was changing. Television was bringing in a new reality that would not fit the "Breakfast With The Johnsons" format. Change was inevitable. But change to what and how to effect it? These were looming questions, posing yet another challenge to the imagination, risk-taking and adventuresomeness that Grandma Dorothea must have somehow sensed years earlier when she declared "Cliffie, you're special.

Reinventing Himself

t was a bittersweet morning in June, 1957, when the final "Breakfast With The Johnsons" aired. More than three thousand programs had filled the ten-year-span since the first program opened with Cliff and family singing *Bless This House*, then ending with the table prayer of thanksgiving. When the final Amen was spoken, a silence followed. Luella broke it with "Some more coffee, Cliff?"—the same (and only) words she spoke on the first broadcast in 1947. Years after the program ended Cliff recalled a summary of the "Breakfast With The Johnsons" decade by noted radio news commentator Paul Harvey. At a local fund raising event he introduced Cliff with the comment that he refereed oatmeal fights at his breakfast table for ten years, got paid for it and when his kids grew up he had to go back to work. Cliff countered with the Harvey signature line "And that's the rest of the story." That was more than a quip, however. There really had to be a rest of the story. Cliff was 42-years-old and without a job. When conversing with his NBC radio friend Dick Johnson of NBC shortly after the Breakfast program ended he was brought up short with Dick Johnson's question to him: "What do you do now as an ex-radio star?" That "ex-radio star" hit home. It was time, once again, to set about the challenge of reinventing himself.

This much was clear. A next career step had to be creatively different. No longer could he build his future in radio around the children. The girls were now into their teens with increasingly crowded school schedules and the desire to outgrow their public image as children around the table. Cliff also knew that Chicago radio was beginning to reflect the changes that were going on in the broadcasting culture throughout America. By late 1957, rock and roll music was taking over the airways and the morning talk shows were adopting the format news, weather, traffic, and sports to fill in between records. Wally Philips was the new fixture at WGN from 6 a.m. He had taken over the "Listen To Cliff" audience and there was no future for Johnson in that time slot. Howard Miller was a counterpart on WIND, which meant that there was no niche left where Cliff had created one previously. He had talked over these matters with Luella. She never prescribed what the next step might be. Her gift was to provide positive commentary and perspective on what had been. Her phrase summing up the "Breakfast With The Johnsons" decade was both affirming and accurate: "It was right for its time." Now the question was what would be right for the new time at hand? That was his task, for which he could count on her total support at his side.

He began the search by contacting trusted friends who knew him and his professional talents well. His first call was to Bill Boyd, the station manager of WLS, the fifty thousand watt station that put it among the strongest in Chicago and the Midwest. Boyd was already mindful of the rapid changes threatening the traditional radio programming that had drawn listeners for decades. That change was forced by the sudden arrival of rock and roll music. Elvis Presley had burst upon the American entertainment scene and WLS felt the aftershock of having to serve up *You Aint Nothin' But A Hound Dog* after years of the Prairie Home Companion. That reality resonated in Boyd's less than comforting words to Cliff: "Most all of us will be out of work before long." The WLS management was in limbo, unsure of how to chart its way through new territory. Boyd's frankness left Johnson with no illusions. He needed to carve out a new career path that would combine two things. It had to be creatively different from all he had known and done in radio heretofore.

Yet it needed to retain Cliff's foremost gift and passion—people connecting, especially with an audience of women.

He had another and new angle on his future. Could he weave real estate into the mix? In l957 the whole Chicago suburban area was exploding with new housing to meet the tide of city dwellers moving out to new communities springing up to the north, west and south of the city. New houses meant new homeowners, most of them younger couples with young children and stay at home moms. Would there not be a new market for a radio audience out there, one that would feature young wives and mothers in newly burgeoning suburbs who could be interviewed from within their own new homes? And wouldn't listeners, primarily the women whose radios were on during the daytime hours, need to know something about mortgages, builders, furnishings and all that goes with building or buying something new? The audience potential was there, as suburbs mushroomed and real estate sales were involved. As a potential sphere for radio programming it was surely an uncrowded field. Cliff was up for giving it his best.

He knew Martin Braun, a respected architect and successful home builder who lived in River Forest. Braun was well connected with key people and currently was serving as president of The Homebuilders Association of Chicago. He invited Cliff to speak at a dinner meeting of that organization with several hundred men and women attending. As Braun introduced Cliff as a man who had talked with people from all walks of life throughout the country and abroad, promoting a wide variety of products and making a national name for himself while making a living at radio. Cliff eyed the couples before him—all of whom were immersed in home building and buying. Bells began ringing in his mind. Here before him was a sample of a new and promising audience. As he spoke he envisioned the possibilities: new homes with new owners in the market for all it takes to buy and furnish a brand new residence. The Braun connection was well worth cultivating as Cliff needed links to a wider network of financial backers to bring his vision to reality. That's what happened. He came into contact with a whole new galaxy of "big boys," as Father Flanagan had put it years earlier. Construction and financial institution leaders such as Edward Shannon of the major Chicago firm of Shannon Lumber and Edward Elbert, president of a nearby Savings and Loan Company as well as president of Lions International were two men who moved in circles that made things happen. Another key participant was Dino Giaccini, an officer in Elbert's savings and loan institution, whose expertise was in finance and mortgage planning. Cliff made good use of his own name value as he won the support of these and other business leaders to stand behind a new venture in radio. Within several weeks of Cliff's speech to the Homebuilders Association the first program was broadcast from a newly built house in Westchester. "Coffee With Cliff" was the name selected for a half hour program.

Meanwhile, Cliff had kept in contact with Bill Boyd of WLS for the purpose of airing "Coffee With Cliff" over that station. Boyd had questions about the whole idea of housewives interviewed in new homes as a sufficient draw for the kind of listening audience he wanted for his fifty thousand watt station. Furthermore, WLS did not offer to secure funding for program. Cliff met that challenge with a proposal of his own. He himself would come up with the $539 advance needed for the broadcast costs each week, something he could manage since he sold the spacious Kenilworth Victorian house no longer needed as the family residence and broadcast studio. He would then broker the half hour program to suburban area stations who in turn would air it in communities of rapidly growing new housing.

It was something WLS had never done and represented a break with their station history of not allowing a broker arrangement for any of their programs. It was also something new for Cliff. He had produced many radio programs. He was new to selling them to smaller stations. It worked with WLS, however, solely because of the Cliff Johnson name and reputation as a respected veteran who knew what he was doing. It worked for Cliff because he worked hard and successfully in a new role as broker of WLS program property to smaller area stations. "Coffee With Cliff" made its debut on September 15, 1957, and was off for a successful two year run. Cliff's main sponsor, Boushelle Rugs, was owned by a man he greatly admired, Cecil Treadway, whose support was more than financial. The Boushelle business location in the city included an auditorium where Treadway himself served several times as a substitute program host for "Coffee With Cliff." He arranged to bus in a hundred or more suburban housewives as an audience, and did everything Cliff did except boom out the Boushelle Rug phone number (Hudson 3-2700) in the catchy commercial that featured the trademark Johnsonian baritone. The favorable audience response drew a growing list of program sponsors whose products and services were tailored to the home buying population. Everything from microwaves to flooring to water softeners to insulation to room furnishings were promoted as Cliff helped housewives share their excitement about moving into the house of their dreams. At the "Coffee With Cliff" debut he had gone to a Jewel Grocery Market for an armload of steaks as a thank-you to the housewives interviewed. Jewel was glad to reap ongoing advertisement benefits by providing steaks gratis for the duration of the program's future. It was programming that met the two-fold criteria Cliff sought in the transition: newness combined with continuity. By one reading it looked like Cliff was still bouncing from one thing to another. By another, however, it was Cliff the independent contractor doing from entrepreneurial necessity what he to do in redirecting his well-honed radio skills toward a new audience of home buyers in expanding suburbs.

Meanwhile another facet of the transition story unfolded. It involved a housing idea unique in the United States in 1957. Commonwealth Edison announced its plan to build a totally new kind of house—completely electric. Cliff had learned of it from his neighbor friend and prominent area realtor, Albert Gloor. The Chicago trade papers had picked up the story, touting it as a harbinger of the house of the future. At that time Cliff had bought an empty lot in River Forest intending to build a family home and was already underway with construction plans. The ComEd house idea triggered in his mind the memories of hosting the "Dream House" program in Lincoln, Nebraska years before. He remembered the powerful attraction that the idea of any new house had, not the least for a daytime radio audience of women. The prospect of being the first family to live in a new house that was all-electric struck him as a plus for his new programming direction. Martin Braun helped him reach the right people at Commonwealth Edison who were actively interested in promoting the concept. To have the first family of Chicago radio as the first occupants was to their advantage. An agreement was reached and construction began. Luella was wary from the start, wondering about the cost of an all-electric house, but was willing to see whether this new place without a chimney would indeed be a dream house or a nightmare of runaway utility costs.

As all of this was happening, out of the blue came a phone call in the late spring of 1958 from Dick Johnson, a good friend and program manager at WMAQ-NBC. He called Cliff's attention to an ad in a travel trade publication that Cliff had, in fact, already noted with interest. Floral Telegraph Delivery, a company with widespread international branches, was looking for a promotional event at the World's Fair soon to open in Brussels, Belgium. An estimated 51 million people from all over the world would be visiting the Fair. Cliff quickly saw the connection of a radio program that would feature the presentation of a corsage or bouquet to some notable Fair visitor, since flowers would certainly be a daily feature in a city and country already famous for flowers. Would Cliff be interested? Cliff was. He quickly got to work on a "Sounds From Europe" program idea and called in his skilled radio engineer and longtime friend, Bill Ketelhut, to handle the technical side of daily five minute spot interviews. Each segment begun with a one line plug for FTD flowers, which fit the tight five-minute program time perfectly well. Before leaving for the twelve-day trip, Cliff pre-recorded five programs and turned the remaining time over to Martin Braun as substitute host on "Coffee With Cliff." Luella stayed home to keep the contractors on schedule at the new Oak Avenue house site. American Express signed on to handle all travel and accommodation arrangements, which insured luxury digs all the way.

The Brussels experience went well. While there Cliff thought of extending the trip eastward to Berlin where "Sounds From Europe" might include sights and sounds from that divided city that had become the dramatic epicenter of the Cold War. He succeeded in making the necessary arrangements, including hiring Werner Dietrich as guide for their interviews in West Berlin alongside the barbed wire divide that would in several years become the most infamous symbol of Communist oppression and isolation, the Berlin Wall. Cliff was intrigued with the possibility of getting through "Checkpoint Charlie," the one access point between East and West Berlin, for interviews with people on the East Berlin side. Bill Ketelhut had brought along the latest in recording devices, an Emerson recorder small enough to be hidden in a wicker basket covered with fruit. Werner Dietrich nixed the idea immediately as too dangerous. He was an ex-German World War II veteran of Russian war prisoner camps who was now a guide for two Americans who were loose in East Berlin with a tape recorder hidden in a fruit basket. Too risky, the German concluded with Germanic finality. But Cliff talked him into a short foray despite the danger, just long enough to get a slice of East Berlin for NBC network listeners back home. The three made it through "Checkpoint Charlie." Among the first people Cliff saw was an older German woman on her way to a market. Through Dietrich the interpreter he learned from her how sparse food was. Even a dollop of lard was two dollars. She let that anecdote serve as a guarded reference to what life was like for her and multitudes more like her. Her concluding words were a surprise. "Trust in God" were three words Cliff did not forget. Just as the interview ended, Dietrich shouted "Get in now!" and shoved both men into the waiting taxi. They had been spotted by the Stasi, the dreaded East German police who were rapidly bearing down on them. With Dietrich shouting at the taxi driver to hit top speed and Johnson and Ketelhut looking anxiously out the back window at the police gaining on them, they barely beat their pursuers to "Checkpoint Charlie." As they slipped through to the West Berlin side, Dietrich pronounced with a sigh of nervous relief that if they would have been caught by the Stasi it would have meant an extended visit in East Berlin "for a long, long, time."

The Paris stop took Cliff back to the Cambon Pension he and the family had enjoyed several years earlier. American Express had arranged a guide for them. A well connected Parisian named Andre Lemaire, who greeted them with elegant French manners and the assurance that when arriving at the Cambon he "would introduce them to the management." That was Lemaire's phrase all over the city, introducing his American guest to people of importance who were in Paris to welcome Charles De Gaulle back from his years of exile in North Africa. Johnson did not succeed in getting an interview with the great man himself, but his guide did arrange contact with two top aides to the General. The final broadcast from Paris was extended to fifteen minutes to cover the stirring pageantry of DeGaulle's victory parade down the Champs Ellyses as all of Paris and much of France turned out to welcome home their wartime hero and most prominent citizen. The only damper on the exciting day of interviews was a telegram from Martin Braun in River Forest: "FLOOD WATERS DISCOVERED UNDER BASEMENT OF NEW HOUSE." The news of a literal damper back home had to do with an unwelcome discovery of a subterranean stream of water under much of the town, including Cliff's site. It wasn't the only news of a cost increase in the Johnson house under construction. The first electric bills were out of sight, as Luella had suspected, running to over a thousand dollars for two months. Cliff hustled back home, well paid for his "Sounds From Europe" and needing every bit of it, even after negotiating a pay rate with

Commonwealth Edison to help meet the utilities cost.

The transition time from the breakfast program to his new directions in his career path covered two years. It was not easy, yet Cliff loved the challenge of it and grew through the experience of brokering radio time, moving into an electric house, promoting new products in a new program and all the while continuing his passion for people-centered radio programming. The pressure of the move kept him on his game and called forth his creative energies in satisfying connections of well tested radio skills to new ways. In the process he developed an appreciation for people who worked the 9 to 5 schedule day in and day out for years. While he sensed the need for professional stability, he knew that the radio world did not provide stability. Everyone had to adopt and adapt—or drop out. Cliff was good at it. He had to be. Along with all of this, he had not lost track of the idea of real estate as a mainstay for future work. The time had arrived for him to actively go after it.

The first step came about during an Oak Park backyard barbecue of a friend in the summer of 1960. In the course of that evening, Cliff met two men who would have a decisive role in his immediate future, Emil Bloche, lawyer and David Decker, realtor; both were men of unquestioned integrity and highly respected in the community. Cliff knew them from various previous associations. He regarded them as two examples of the "big boy" stature ala Father Flanagan, but this time the phrase signaled moral soundness and community contribution rather than celebrity status. As the evening progressed, Cliff chatted with Decker who had been a longtime radio fan of the Johnsons and a great admirer of Luella. He commented on Cliff's new radio venture with a casual reference to "…all those new houses in what used to be cornfields," and added, almost as an afterthought, "Cliff, did you ever think about getting into real estate?" Of course, Cliff had been thinking about exactly that for some time, and was only too happy to hear Decker add, "Come over to the office sometime and let's talk about it." It was a casual comment that Cliff took with more than casual interest. He did pursue the invitation by stopping by at the Decker office at 1119 Pleasant in Oak Park. It was a splendid building, located near downtown Oak Park, a prime location. The Decker first floor offices contained twenty of the most spacious and desirable apartment units west of the Chicago Loop. When David Decker, the building owner and respected realtor nearing retirement, suggested a talk about a real estate future, it was a golden opportunity. And Cliff, now in his mid-forties and headlong into a career change, was quick to seize it. The conversation that soon followed was productive. It included Luella, who shared Cliff's interest and acumen for real estate work. Both of them got the study materials and in a matter of a month had their real estate license, plus access to the Decker office location for half days during the week. It could not have been a more fortuitous beginning.

Radio remained in his blood, however. The fascination with communicating over the sounds waves that had gripped him as a second grader had not faded with the turn to real estate. He still kept up with the radio trade magazines and had his eye open to anything new that might come along. Which it did early in 1962. He spotted a small ad announcing a pioneering venture that caught his attention immediately. For the first time anywhere an all news station was about to begin. An experienced radio veteran from Texas, Gordon McClendon, had purchased WYNR, a small Chicago station located in the transmitter tower house at 79th and Kedzie on Chicago's south side. Cliff couldn't resist. He made an audition tape and send it off. In short order he had the job as producer and later program director at WNUS. In March, 1963, he aired the first daylong program that featured nothing but news, twenty-four hours a day, seven days a week. McClendon hired eight other announcers to form the staff of twelve needed for the eight hour shifts. The idea took off famously. Within a year the upstart all news station from a South Side Chicago warehouse was pushing past the major Chicago stations for top ratings in the radio news market. By late 1963 McClendon had developed WYNR into the larger WNUS all-news station, with the Chicago giant WBBM going all news not long after. The larger station adopted the format Cliff had developed lock, stock and barrel. The WNUS staff had grown to twelve announcers as the ratings rose, all of whom decided to wage a strike for a larger share of the all-news bonanza. Cliff rode out the labor dispute and in 1964 was moved up to interim managing editor and the manager of sales, the position he preferred as the burden of the real estate work and commuting to the all news station was exhausting. He divided his working schedule half-time with WNUS until 1968, the year that WBBM went all news on a fifty-thousand-watt signal that proved too much competition for the smaller station.

Again, timing was providential for Cliff. As the radio work moved to the sidelines in 1968, Cliff's good friend, David Decker was acting upon his plans to retire, already several years in the making. He saw, especially in Luella and Cliff an effective business team that could flourish in real estate even as they had as radio parents around the breakfast table. Decker was confident that the gold-plated realtor reputation he had built over the years would fare well under the Johnsons. When he suggested that they take it over, adding that all he wanted was "a thousand dollars on the barrel head and a hundred dollars a month rent" for the prime office location fully furnished, they were as overwhelmed with gratitude as they were eager to prove worthy of the extraordinary offer. The LuCliff Realities team was formed in 1967 with a new logo, a new staff and new energies to continue the Decker reputation that had an anchor of integrity in the community.

There was something else intriguing about the LuCliff move into the office. It had two entrances and space inside for more than one real estate office. Once again, a visionary idea clicked in Cliff's mind. Why not a travel office to accommodate that extra entrance and the space inside? The idea was not entirely novel. In the late 1950's Cliff had done a great deal of travel within the United States and in Europe. He had widespread contacts with corporations such as American Express, Eastern Airlines, United Airlines, railroads, major steamship lines and hotels in America and Europe. A travel office was the best idea for using the extra entrance and added space. He and Luella applied themselves once again to the preparatory study required to open a specialized business. The National Board of Transportation and the Air Traffic Corporation set rigorous standards for the sale of air and train travel tickets. He and Luella boned up on the regulatory materials and passed the test required before the Cliff Johnson Travel Agency could be chartered late in 1969.

The ATC also required a $20,000 amount up front in escrow before it could grant its authorization to sell travel, which was ten thousand dollars more than the Johnsons had. Cliff went to one bank and stated his case—unsuccessfully. The pressure to come up with the second ten thousand was enough to motivate him to make another try, this time at the Avenue Bank of Oak Park. He had met the president, Carl Oberwortmann, on a number of community event occasions, but did not know him well. Undaunted, he made an appointment with the bank president and made his case in one long, rambling, and somewhat desperate sentence: "Mr. Oberwortmann, it's true I don't know you well personally but I have ten thousand dollars to begin a new travel agency in my new office at Dave Decker's former location and I am here to ask you for the ten thousand dollar loan I need to meet the twenty thousand necessary to start a new business that my wife and I will run successfully!" Oberwortmann greeted the bold proposition with silence for a full twenty seconds, looking Johnson straight in the eye. Then he spoke. "Get over to my loan officer, Ade Berg, and have him write it up for you before I change my mind." The deal was done and neither Avenue Bank nor Cliff Johnson ever regretted the transaction. Oberwortmann's response made it clear that the Cliff Johnson name had lost none of its punch a decade after the breakfast program had ended.

The 1970's proved to be good years for LuCliff Realtors and the Cliff

Johnson Travel Agency. As the businesses grew, so did the need for larger office locations. How they came to be is narrative of quirky happenstance, luck and quick actions to make things happen. All these occurred in no orderly schedule, but as events woven into the daily schedule of hard work and heads-up attentiveness to what was going on around them. The travel business took a long step forward when the Johnson Agency landed the bookings for two-hundred-fifty certified public accountants for a conference in Bermuda. Cliff worked a favorable charter travel contract with Eastern Airlines and Holiday Inn in Bermuda which was enough to pay off nearly the total bank loan needed to start the business two years earlier. That turn of events increased the Johnson Travel Agency business considerably, making it plausible to think of another more centrally located business address for the growing volume of travel business. Cliff's contacts with Oak Park Trust and Saving Bank vice-president Donald Sandro and his computer trained assistant, William Langley. These two successfully persuaded the bank board of directors and president, Wallace Austin, to set up a travel agency space for Cliff in a lobby area off a side entrance at 1048 Lake Street. A prime location at the hub of the business community. Included in the arrangement was a ticket counter offering Cliff Johnson Travel Agency materials and services. That, however, turned the bank entranceway into a maze of racks packed with travel literature, improvised stools, and small benches for customers. It was a boon for the travel agency. It wasn't long before the bottom line had quadrupled because of the key location attracting bank customers and shoppers passing by the bank corner. But it was not ideal for the bank staff. The water-cooler rumors that "Cliffie's Travel Agency" was becoming a problem soon reached the Johnsons. They were hardly surprised, then, when bank president Wallace Austin sauntered by the crowded travel counter, drawing generously on his ever-present pipe and through the billows of smoke delivering his soft-toned ultimatum: "Don't you think it's getting a little crowded in here?" A move was inevitable, but where could Cliff and Luella afford a location that desirable?

Once again, Cliff drew on key friends to help him find an answer. John Pilgrim was a community realtor of long experience, another one who Father Flanagan would place in the "big boys" category. Cliff sought him out, knowing that Pilgrim was managing the three story apartment building across from the street from the bank. The first floor levels housed small businesses, among them a barber shop. Dropping in on Pilgrim, Cliff started with the casual query "How are things going?" Shaking his head, Pilgrim spoke of the changing times in which small businesses couldn't make it in the high rent neighborhood anymore. Continuing the lament, he cited the barber shop as an example of the craziness of the changing times. Pilgrim, well past his middle years, noted that younger men are going for longer hair styles and barbers who were not into longer styles were suffering. As an example he cited the shop Cliff was interested in. Johnson picked up the cue and shifted the subject to the lease situation at 161 Marion Street. Keeping to his ethical code, Pilgrim refused to give any information, but suggested that Cliff might want to talk the subject over with the barber himself. He wasted no time in doing so.

On a spring day he told Luella that he was off to the barber shop. She noted an unusual ring of enthusiasm in his announcement, plus the fact that he didn't need a haircut. Haircuts were a subject they often joked about, especially when recalling the South Dakota days when all it took was a bowl on the head in the farm kitchen and an even cut all around. Cliff found the barber shop door open as he approached and found the barber sitting alone in the three chair shop. The conversation began with typical barbershop small talk, but then turned into more than an hour visit as the barber chose that time and place to air his dilemma. He knew he had to move to lower his business costs, yet wanted to keep his customers by staying in the neighborhood. Cliff asked if there was anyplace he had in mind. Yes, he answered, there was Dino's, a shop not more than three blocks away. Cliff suggested they go together to Marion and Chicago and talk with the prospective partner. Cliff helped him make his proposal, which—amazingly—succeeded on the spot. The barber and Cliff reached an agreement on the sale of his shop location before they were back at the 161 Marion address. He returned to tell Luella about the rapid succession of events, adding that it was an eighteen-hundred-dollar haircut that didn't include the chairs but secured a new home for their travel business. Her response was a flash of her ready wit: "At least you didn't get clipped." It was one of those quirky, serendipitous events which was perfectly timed for the move from the bank lobby to a favorable business address that was later expanded to include the office next door. Cliff Johnson Travel was now well positioned for growth toward annual gross sales which would reach the three million dollar mark by the late 1980's.

By the late 1970's Cliff had invested much of his working time to the travel business and became president of the Midwest Agents Selling Travel organization. In early 1978 he noted a Chicago Tribune article on President Jimmy Carter's proposal of tourism as a means of re-opening relations with Cuba. All travel had been shut down for nearly two decades following the Bay of Pigs fiasco in 1959. In response to that article, a Chicago travel office called Cliff informing him that a booking exclusively for travel agents had been made on a Caribbean cruise ship, the Daphne, currently docked in New Orleans and possibly headed for Cuba. Would he go as the Midwest Agents organization leader? Fidel Castro had let it be known that any news journalists would be forbidden entry, but travel agents were welcome because Castro needed the dollars that American tourist trade might bring in. Another item of unusual interest was Castro's wish that the notable American journalist, Barbara Walters, was to fly in as a special guest. Why Walters? Castro alone knew. But Cliff took on the challenge and with Luella's blessing flew to New Orleans to join the Daphne passengers. After a three-day wait, made quite bearable by the presence of jazz greats Dizzy Gillespie and Earl "Fatha" Hines on board as part of the Cuba-America cultural exchange, the Daphne set sail for Havana with ten travel agents on board, Cliff included. Before docking, a Cuban government boat brought inspectors on board who gave all ten a grilling before issuing landing permits. Cliff said nothing about his newsman career but as president of the travel agents group passed muster. He, Barbara Walters and the others were overwhelmed by the sight of thousands of Cubans at the dock to welcome the first Americans in 20 years. Upon setting foot on shore, Cliff broke ranks and had a bystander use his camera for a picture with a cluster of smiling Cubans surrounding him. The snapshot made the NBC Nightly News with Chet Huntley and David Brinkley as well as the next issue of *Time Magazine*. Barbara Walters arrived by air and sat beside Fidel Castro in the lead Jeep of the parade, a sight that also made headlines throughout the United States. The Cuba stay covered a week of strictly controlled visits to approved sites. Cliff's guide, who explained that he was "Fidel's brother" balked at Cliff's request to visit Ernest Hemingway's cottage a few miles out of Havana and off the official itinerary. A twenty dollar bill solved that problem, and Cliff was driven to the beachside house made famous by Hemingway in his *Old Man And The Sea*. The place was locked up. But Cliff found a bathroom window unlocked and with the help of the guide who was anxiously looking out in all directions, hauled himself through the opening and took several dozen photographs before exiting the way he entered. No one was the wiser and Cliff kept mum on the experience until he was safely back on homeland soil.

A meaningful career shift had been successfully maneuvered from 1957, which saw the conclusion of "Breakfast With The Johnsons" and the move into a different radio format, a real estate business established, and a travel agency started with promise for the future. Creative imagination, combined with hard work, the help of good friends and the attending angels made it happen. The family had found a solid spiritual home at Grace Lutheran Church and an abiding friendship with the pastor. The children were growing into new phases of their lives and through the determined efforts of Luella and Cliff were spared the blight of turning into spoiled celebrity brats. Cliff and Luella continued to team up effectively in new business ventures which put their best qualities to work.

Cliff had escaped a prolonged stay in East Germany. The family was at home at a new River Forest address with plenty of electricity and the bills to go with it. The business locations had moved from a Victorian home studio, to an ample real estate office, to a bank lobby, to a former barber shop and nothing had been lost throughout the moves. Life was good as the Johnsons ventured with all Americans into an era of unprecedented change, peril, and promise. Vietnam, long hair styles, the drug culture, rock and roll, the sexual revolution were among the volatile changes coursing through the land, assaulting the institutions of family and marriage as never before in American life. In new ways and under more demanding circumstances, the prayer that had begun the breakfast table program each morning for ten years would need continued praying: "Bless this house, O Lord we pray, Make it strong by night and day…"

Grandmother
Dorthea Johnson
(front row center)
Cliff's Dad *(2nd
from left back row)*
South Dakota
1902

Cliff *(center)* with family ready to
sing in church.
1920

Cliff with
his brother
Joseph and
pony Nellie
1927

Cliff in the studio *1939*

Cliff with his bride Luella
Cliff says "She is gorgeous!"
1938

Up there with the
Big Boys Home—
Kenilworth Avenue,
Oak Park, Illinois
1949

The Cliff
Johnson Family
on the Streets
of Paris—
"Operation
Hometown
America—
Oak Park"
1955

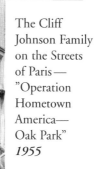

The Johnson Family
backstage at the Warner
Theatre in New York with
Abbott & Costello
1953

Cliff interviewing Orson
Wells in Omaha, Nebraska
1939

Luella wearing her Easter
bonnet on 5th Avenue,
New York chatting with
Mike Wallace
1953

at the CBS Studios in
Omaha, Nebraska with
Glenn Miller and singer
Marion Hutton
1940

Good friend, Earl Warren, Governor of California & Chief Justice United States Supreme Court
1947

Father Flanagan of Boys Town, Nebraska. Close Friend and Mentor to Cliff
1939

George Burns and Gracie Allen Omaha, Nebraska
1940

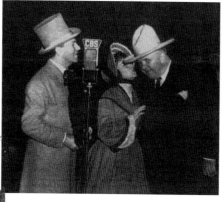

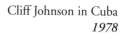

The first family home on Woodbine Avenue in Oak Park, Illinois
1947

Cliff Johnson in Cuba
1978

CHAPTER 7

New Gains, Grievous Loss

hroughout the 1970's and '80's, international travel opportunities were on the rise as Cliff took on leadership positions in two professional travel organizations: The
American Federation of Travel Agencies Midwest Chapter
(ASTA) and The Midwest Agents Selling Travel (MAST). In the course
of preparing and making these trips, it was always a welcome surprise to
come across former listeners to the breakfast programs whose memories
of the Johnson clan had not dimmed over the several decades since the
program ended.

Among the more memorable instances was Francis Goranin, an Austrian
Jew who was among the fortunate ones who had escaped his homeland
before the Nazi occupation. One day he simply slung his skis over his
shoulder and instead of going skiing, slipped across the border to
Switzerland and finally to the United States where he settled in
Springfield, Illinois. There he became an early fan of "Breakfast With
The Johnsons," making them virtually a substitute family for his own,
which, like so many Jews, he had to leave behind. He was heading toward
a pharmaceutical career when he discovered that his multi-lingual talents
made him better suited for the travel business which was expanding in
the years following World War II. With his background of European
contacts he quickly became the rising star of Vega International Travel,

and eventually became president and owner of the firm. By the mid-1970's his stature in the industry was indicated by his election as the national president of The American Society of Travel Agents.

Cliff had met him during his term as president of ASTA and when introducing himself by name was delighted to hear Goranin exclaim in his German flavored English, "So, you are the Cliff Johnson mit all dose kids I used to hear all the time on the radio venn I vas verking in the drug store!" Cliff was even more delighted when Goranin, well wired to so many key people and places all over Europe, organized the needed contacts for his trip to Berlin in October, 1990. As an ASTA leader, he took a delegation of travel agents to the city for the formal opening of free travel from East to West Germany with ceremonies also celebrating the first anniversary of the fall of the Berlin Wall. Cliff and Luella, together with her sister, Betty, joined the huge throng of East and West Berliners streaming down the famed *Unter den Linden Strasse* toward the Brandenburg Gate, belly to back, tears on their faces as they heard the loudspeakers boom out Beethoven's, *Ode to Joy,* from his Ninth Symphony. The thrill of seeing Germans separated since 1945 now coming together freely was an unforgettable emotional high. It added to the power of the moment that Goranin, the Jewish refugee, one-time radio fan and now international travel executive, had reconnected with the Johnsons and set up the arrangements for the travelers and their travel agent companions. After Berlin and visits to the Martin Luther sites in Wittenberg and surrounding cities, Cliff and Luella traveled northward to the Island of Fehmarn, just off the German coast in the Baltic Sea. where Luella's mother had been born. They found the familial house in the old European style of family quarters on one end of the dwelling, the livestock on the other. The visit was especially poignant for Luella. She was the first of her maternal family to return from America for a visit since the late 19th century migration. Her mother's death in 1949 was a grievous loss; seeing where Dorothea Tanck had begun her early life brought a healing balm for those wounds.

Luella's companionship on most of the international travels provided numerous occasions when her unabashed wonder at it all would surface. Along with all the sophistication and common sense that came naturally to her she could not cease marveling over the fact that she and Cliff could come from their Dakota prairie roots to see so much of the world and meet so many people of so many varied backgrounds and interests. On their first trip to Mexico in the early 1970's, Luella was glued to the window as the plane banked in preparation for landing in Acapulco. Commenting on the beauty of the mountains below she turned to Cliff and said, a bit wide-eyed with wonder, "This reminds me a little of the Black Hills!" Cliff agreed, but added as a native South Dakotan that there were no signs of any Mexican counterparts to the Mt. Rushmore faces of Washington, Jefferson, Lincoln and Roosevelt.

As president of the The American Society of Travel Agents Midwest Chapter, it was customary for Cliff to have a limousine waiting at airport destinations. When Luella accompanied him to Cairo on her first visit to Egypt in 1983, she was not quite prepared for the sleek black limo ready for them at the Cairo airport and the uniformed driver's greeting to Cliff: "Welcome, Mr. President, to Cairo." The Mr. President title was one he frankly enjoyed, yet he could never hear himself addressed as Mr. President without wondering if it was he who was being addressed. Though an owner of two successful businesses as well as a travel industry leader, he never saw himself entirely free from the lingering baggage of the college dropout from Sioux Falls, the son who didn't go on into the pastoral ministry. It was gratifying, of course, to be met at the Cairo airport by a chauffeured limo and driven through the dusty chaos of Cairo traffic in air conditioned comfort, to be wined and dined in a luxury hotel and enjoy the pyramids and other antiquities with expert guides attending to every detail. At the same time it was to the credit of both of them that along with their sophistication as world travelers they could still marvel that they could be doing these things without losing touch with their prairie roots and the worldview that went with it. Luella's comment on the red carpet welcome in Cairo revealed that quality when she settled into the limo back seat beside Cliff, leaned over and asked, smilingly, "Do you think we should be doing this?" Cliff answered with a knowing pat of her hand, "Soak it up, my dear. It won't last too long."

Together with their traveling entourage of thirty travel agents, they were booked at the Continental Hotel for the five day visit. Cliff kept thinking who in the city he should meet and how could he bring it off. At supper one evening in the hotel he learned that Mrs. Anwar Sadat, the widow of the assassinated president of Egypt, was speaking to an audience of dignitaries several floors above. He asked a fellow travel agent if he had any idea of how he could meet Mrs. Sadat and ask her down for a brief greeting to the ASTA delegates. His friend responded that those were ideas the president should come up with. Hearing that, he made his way to the fifth floor room where Mrs. Sadat was the guest of honor. Cliff presented his credentials as ASTA president as well as his Rotary Club ID to the officials guarding the door, which proved good enough get his note of invitation passed on to Jehan Sadat. Upon finishing her speech and sitting down, the strikingly beautiful widow of the late president, ever gracious as well as shrewdly aware of the value of American tourist dollars, read the note with Cliff's request, agreed to it and accompanied Cliff downstairs to the American guests for words of welcome and well-wishing. The travel agents were properly impressed by their president's finesse in securing an impromptu appearance by the ex-president's widow. The moment was a highlight of the Cairo stay.

Four years later another international convention of ASTA took them to Spain. In Madrid, Luella joined Cliff during a timeout from conference sessions for a shopping visit to a Lladro ceramic art shop, and was quite taken with the beauty of the pieces on display. Cliff stood back to watch as she gingerly took in hand each piece for a closer look at the understated gracefulness of the Lladro artistic style. Seeing her wide-eyed but reticent to do more than look, he took a deep breath and announced: "Go

ahead, my dear, . . . have fun." She made the best of the offer before any
change of mind might break the spell. As the items of her choosing began
to collect on the counter, the clerk became as wide-eyed as Luella. "Do
you have a shop back home?" she asked. Not so, Luella replied, her mind
already envisioning the placement of each piece in the Johnson household. The Lladro art works became a treasured reminder of the Madrid
stopover on the Spain and Majorca trip and remained so until Luella's
final illness, when she designated each piece for each of her children
shortly before her death.

In Jerusalem another occasion arose when the capacity for amazement in
both Cliff and Luella took a different form. This time it was the respectful silence that comes with an awareness of being present to people in a
city filled with survivors of one of the greatest tragedies of history, the
Holocaust. After several days of visiting the sacred sites in Jerusalem and
Bethlehem, they were guests of Teddy Kollek, the mayor of Jerusalem. As
Cliff and Luella sat down at the luncheon table, Kollek began the conversation with an invitation to tell him something of themselves. Cliff
reminisced about his early days in radio and mentioned the importance
of his Father Flanagan and "Boys Town" connection. The mention of
"Boys Town" brought an immediate response from the mayor as the fame
of the Omaha program for boys without a home and family had spread
all the way to Jerusalem. Kollek explained that he had already laid the
groundwork for a start in something similar himself. He described his
vision of a Boys Of Jerusalem counterpart and was in discussion with the
Roman Catholic Archdiocese of Jerusalem with plans to bring it about.
It was a good start to the luncheon conversation as Cliff was pleased to
bring valued information that quickly moved the conversation from
polite table talk to a project high on the list of Mayor Kollek's priorities.

But something more memorable to the Johnsons was to come. Another
American guest around the table was Chicagoan Mark Berkman, the
owner of a major travel agency in Chicago. He was a Jewish refugee, who,

like Francis Goranin, had been born in Poland and fled the country before the Nazi Holocaust drove millions of Jews to the ovens of Auschwitz. After hearing Cliff's "Boys Town" recollections, Kollek turned the conversation to the prickly issues of Jewish-Arab relations in the city and beyond. He began diplomatically with a question, "Do you know anything about us?" and followed it up with a sweeping overview of Jewish history and the more recent events that led to the formation of the State of Israel in 1948. Cliff and Luella sensed that at this point in the conversation it was their place to be eavesdroppers more than contributors. The moment belonged to Berkman who responded to Kollek's leading question with an impassioned account of his own family's ordeal of suffering, survival, flight from the death camps and finally starting life from scratch as refugees in a new land. As Berkman poured out his personal story, Kollek responded with corresponding narratives of Jews who had come home to Israel after repression and loss in many parts of the world. That, said Kollek, was what comprised the backbone of Israeli resolve and accounted for their determination to make a Jewish homeland worthy of all the centuries of enduring and praying by Jews who could only long for this day without seeing it fulfilled. Cliff and Luella found the conversation intense and memorable as they sat for several hours with a key figure in the huge and complex task of bringing Jerusalem closer to its Hebrew meaning, the *City of Peace*. Long after that day Cliff kept in mind the words with which Mayor Kollek concluded the conversation: "After wandering the world for so many centuries, we Jews are at home...but we're not yet home." They were an affirmation of nearly four millennia of Jewish history as well as an acknowledgment of the agonizing difficulty of being a peaceful city in a morass of hate and violence on all sides.

Another ASTA international conference took them to one of the most beautiful coastal cities anywhere, Dubrovnik on the Adriatic in what is now Croatia. A meeting of the board of directors was among the events scheduled early in the conference. World travel leaders are good at selecting choice sites for board meetings; the location was a patio situated on a mountain side with the deep blue waters of the Adriatic spread out before them. It was the customary to begin the meeting by going around the table with each giving his name plus a sentence or two about where he came from. Cliff's turn came: "I am Cliff Johnson from Oak Park, Illinois, the home of Ernest Hemingway, Frank Lloyd Wright, and Cliff Johnson." Smiles of approval all around the table as the board members took in the trio of names. Then one colleague from Milan, Italy added with a straight face, "Who are the other two guys?"

Travel opportunities overseas during the years from the early 1970's through 1990 broadened the Johnsons and gave them a window onto the rapidly changing international world. It was essential for their travel business, of course, but it was more than that. It gave Cliff new level of administrative leadership experience in domestic and international travel organizations, together with further moments of double-take when addressed as Mr. President. Luella kept intact her unflappable cool and genuine wonder at the sheer beauty of the earth and its far reaches. They enjoyed the welcome surprises of radio fans turning up in unexpected times and places. They had the fun of doing all this together. They shared the experiences of people and places near and far that were the stuff of lasting memories. This good fortune did not come to many couples. Though they worked hard for it, they were aware of the uniqueness of what was given them and they savored it with gratitude.

Throughout these decades in the travel business, real estate was no less a part of the Johnson business team, in fact real estate was their major source of income. As early as 1965 Cliff had been elected to the local board of realtors and served as public relations chairman for twenty years. He fulfilled that role in various ways, including a regular column on local housing trends in connection with the LuCliff newspaper ads. Public relations became an increasingly serious matter as the issue of racial integration moved more and more to the forefront in Oak Park, a community of

65,000 residents bordered on the east by the Austin neighborhood of Chicago which was in the midst of the full scale convulsion of a predominantly white area turning nearly all black in the space of a few years in the middle 1950's. By 1960 the stage was set for yet one more replay of white flight with all the attending forces of real estate redlining, racial stereotyping and violence. Less than 1% of Oak Park was black in 1960 and the adjoining upscale River Forest could count its minority residents on one hand. Before the 1950's ended the battle lines between pro and anti integration forces were drawn. The Oak Park home of the distinguished black scientist, Dr. Percy Julian, had been fire bombed twice. It was not clear who did the bombing, but there was little doubt that the vast majority in Oak Park and River Forest, while uncomfortable with fire bombings and the image it portrayed (Hemingway had once characterized Oak Park as a town of broad lawns and narrow minds and the sting still lingered), were more uncomfortable with having to face the facts of racial prejudice. The prevailing mood was simply to wish the Julians would move elsewhere and let sleeping dogs lie locally.

But there were also Oak Parkers who thought otherwise and were ready to do something positive about it. Signs of that courageous mindset began to appear through letters to the town newspapers, clergy association calls for racial justice in sermons and congregation forums, and civics classroom discussions in the schools. And not to be omitted from the list was the "Breakfast With the Johnsons" radio program itself which dealt with the realities of racial prejudice head-on via the unedited conversations of the Johnson kids who were classmates of the Julian kids. These early signs of hope for integration rather than white flight were important, but there was another group that held greater tipping point potential for which direction the community would go.

At the cross hairs of the problem were the realtors. Cliff was among them and heard, saw and felt the uneasiness running through the community. From his second floor real estate office overlooking Oak Park's central business corner at Lake and Marion streets he was in a pivotal location to grasp the commercial and social implications of which force would prevail, inclusion or exclusion. Within his line of sight he could see Marshall Fields and Montgomery Wards, the giant anchor stores that made Oak Park the choice shopping center for the western suburbs in the 1960's. Up and down the street were the retail shops and boutiques that were trendsetters for the future. All this and more was at stake. The watchword of the realtors and business leaders was that Oak Park was the place to live and shop. But for whom? Was it merely sloganeering that added an unspoken footnote that barred people of color? Or was there enough moral backbone behind it to make it a platform for the hard work of confronting the deep seated racism that lurked just below the surface of civility. Cliff and Luella, along with all the other realtors of Oak Park, were familiar enough with the code language on the street that was hardly subtle: "Sell before the market goes down when the blacks start coming into our village… Stay away from the south side of Oak Park—that's where the blacks are going to hit… The blacks won't be able to handle the taxes in north Oak Park—that's where it's safe… We're getting out now and heading for Oak Brook—just like the big Oak Park stores are doing."

Some realtors risked little to counter that mindset. But others did. Among those who exercised a quiet but critically important influence of positive realism on his professional colleagues was John Pilgrim. He had the right credentials as a son of a distinguished Oak Park family of pioneers in the realty market. He was respected by his peers as successful, business savvy and visionary. He combined principle with a pragmatism that made realtors listen when he spoke. Cliff recalled his words at a luncheon meeting of the Oak Park Board of Realtors: "This too shall pass. We can work this out. Panic is not the answer. We can resolve this challenge with rational action. There is a place for black people and all colors in this village." These were gutsy words at a time of peak racial tensions in the struggle for civil rights throughout the nation. Martin Luther King had recently led a march through Cicero, the bastion of belligerent defiance against any prospective black resident. Soon Chicago's west side would join the ranks of other American cities going up in flames after King's assassination. Pilgrim and the realtors who followed his counsel were not out in the streets protesting bigotry. They were fulfilling a role that was largely behind the scenes, one that put them at the key juncture of realtors working with customers, helping to tilt the transaction toward fairness and a racially integrated stability instead of caving in to stereotypical prejudice that eventually made things worse for everybody. Cliff and Luella, both licensed brokers, felt the sting of accusations from the anti-integration people. They were caricatured as illegal counselors for managed integration in Oak Park. But, with other realtors sufficient in number to help stave off the fearful ones, stayed the course laid out by John Pilgrim and helped pull the pendulum toward making Oak Park one of the most successfully integrated Chicago suburbs throughout the 70's and 80's. The Oak Park-River Forest High School population of 30% black students by the 1990's indicated how far the town had come in forty years of struggle.

Years later those efforts paid an unexpected dividend. In 1994 Anna Julian, the widow and intellectual partner of her late husband Percy Julian, a woman of distinction in her own right, was honored on her 90th birthday. The occasion was an awards banquet sponsored by the Oak Park and River Forest Family Service and Mental Health Agency. It was held at the Oak Park Country Club where four decades earlier, ironically enough, a person of color could not even work in the locker room, much less sit down for a meal in the same dining room where the elegant black-tie event took place. Cliff Johnson was the master of ceremonies for the evening. After the cocktail hour and meal, he warmed up the audience with stories of his own, as well as a call for hands-up volunteers to add their own anecdotes of tribute to Anna and the Julian clan. Knowing Cliff well, Anna had asked him during the dinner if he was going to tell Percy's favorite story. Cliff assured her it was coming. The background for the story was the pre-Civil War era when slaves in the American south escaped northward in wagon loads of wood, piled high but stacked in such a way that a small hiding place was preserved for the runaway slave. Thus the popular line of vulgar jargon: "there's a nigger in the woodpile." Percy Julian had this twist on the phrase, which Cliff knew well and saved as the concluding punch line for the evening. The story began with breakfast time at the stately Percy Julian home in Oak Park. Julian was on the back porch savoring the early fall morning air. Anna called him to come in for breakfast. He responded by telling her to hurry outside. She did so, fearing something bad had happened. There stood Percy, chuckling as he pointed to his neighbor, Mr. Goelitz, borrowing some of his stacked fireplace wood. "Would you look at that, Anna" he declared. "There's a white man in my woodpile." A hesitant titter broke the silence following the punch line, then rose into a crescendo of hearty laughter and applause as the point sank in. It was the perfect closer to a memorable evening, with many of Oak Park's elite able to laugh at themselves. It could not have happened without a host of community forces of good will at work, overtly and covertly, for the previous forty years. Among the realtors of the town that had helped that happen was Cliff, now without Luella at his side, and struggling to put together a new way of life following her death in 1993.

Luella's first signs of pancreatic cancer came in the summer of 1991 when patches of jaundice appeared on her body and in her eyes. With her typical directness, the oldest daughter Sandra commented that her mother's eyes didn't look right. With her equally candid stiff upper lip response, Luella dismissed it as something she ate. It was not dismissable, however, as the jaundice did not disappear. On the afternoon of July 3 Cliff took her to the office of their physician, Dr. Harry Swanstrom. He was not there however. A younger colleague examined Luella while Cliff sat outside in the waiting room. The doctor called him in. As he entered the office and saw the expression on Luella's face he was hit by the first hint of what was coming. The doctor spoke with a blunt, clinical finality: "Luella has cancer of the pancreas. She has perhaps ninety days to live."

Both were stunned. Luella was admitted that afternoon for three days of further tests at West Suburban Hospital in Oak Park. It was time enough for both of them to gather their resources for the coming life and death battle. Cliff called in his family as well as his pastor at Grace Church to confer on a strategy of defiant resistance. The Johnsons were not inclined to adopt a course of passive despair, but had no immediate knowledge of where to turn. It was providential that during Luella's hospital stay they happened to bump into Judy Stein, a fellow parishioner of Grace and medical staff person at the hospital. When she heard of their dilemma she immediately recommended a consultation visit to Dr. Sudershan Gopal Rao, an internist in Racine, Wisconsin, who had mastered a new technique for treating pancreatic cancer. It was a difficult procedure consisting of the insertion of a stent down the windpipe past the lungs, connecting to the pancreatic area where a powerful new medicinal injection went to work holding back the spread of the disease. The drive to Racine covering several months and a half dozen trips were bittersweet for both. They were grateful for Dr. Rao. His professional expertise and gentle manner spurred their hope for at least a prolonging of Luella's days if not a cure for the disease. But the they knew that they were not only traveling to Racine but journeying through the valley and shadow of death as well. That awareness coupled with her weakened condition made talking too much physical effort. They spent the two hour drive up and back mostly in silence, occasionally clasping each other's hand, leaving unspoken the things of the heart that were too deep for words.

The Rao treatment regimen did bring swift relief. The jaundice disappeared shortly after her final treatment. Luella did not die in ninety days. Though weakened, she recovered well enough by the summer of 1993 to keep a light schedule around the house. Above all, she summoned enough strength for what was her last major event outside the house, and it was one she would not miss despite her illness. In June of that year she was among those cheering when Concordia University President George Heider placed the Bachelor of Arts diploma into the hands of her 77 year old husband. More than anyone else present she knew what that moment meant to Cliff. It brought a closure laden with Divine grace to his self-imposed burden of carrying the college dropout baggage since leaving Augustana College in 1936. It was a triumph for her as well, that she was still alive to share that happy day with him and the family. The months following, however, were a downhill slide into a metastasized spread of the disease. At no point along that hard way did her faith waver or her composure dissolve into complaints or bitterness. "Read to me" was her daily request. Cliff, her children, her pastor and closest friends did so, coming often to her bedside to read Biblical passages and hymn verses that were treasures from her childhood. In assembling a series of Scripture passages during that time, Cliff discovered for himself the incomparable power of the Gospel of Christ's victory over death and the withdrawal of death's sting through the resurrection hope bestowed by Christ's resurrection. The witness of Luella's faith through her final battle bolstered him for lonely days ahead as well as a transition to a congregational participation in worship and service at a deeper level than ever before in his adult life. It also inspired him later to record and publish *Passages To Peace,* a compact disc recording of the passages once read to Luella now offered to a larger audience.

Luella Goss Johnson died on December 4, 1993. The funeral service at Grace Church was a celebration of her 78 years of faith, active in love as a spouse, mother, grandmother and friend whose qualities of mind and spirit reflected what the Apostle Peter named as "the lasting beauty of a gentle and quiet spirit, which is very precious in God's sight" (I Peter 3:4). Cliff carried her ashes in his lap as his grandson drove the car in the funeral procession to the cemetery. He placed them himself in the grave opening. In the moment of silence kept by her family and friends as the committal prayers ended, there was already a sense forming that the memories of her innate goodness and the durability of her legacy of faith could not be confined to the small space in the earth that enclosed her ashes.

In ways, both personal and public, Cliff discovered new applications of the Biblical truth that the good works of the faithful indeed do follow them—sometimes as the blessing of a needed shakeup. As often happens when wives precedes their husbands in death, Cliff found that his journey through grief was made the more difficult because he, like many widowers, became neglectful in taking care of himself with proper diet and the most rudimentary housekeeping habits. Within a year of her death he found himself hurrying through supper while standing at the kitchen sink with cooking pots and opened cans subbing for the little used dinner plates on the shelf. Among Luella's good works that followed her were mealtimes meant to savor and enjoy, and recalling her standards brought the needed shakeup. He found another way to fight through the loneliness felt, especially at mealtimes, by fixing a balanced supper, sitting down at a properly set table and lighting the candles for the touch of class that would make Luella smile in approval. In this hardest transition of his life, he grew in a self-awareness that Luella would surely have affirmed. He did not need to be wherever the big boys were in order to be up to what was required for this new time in his life. He was the big boy himself. That way of putting it, however, was fully inadequate for the spiritual renewal into which Cliff was being led, step by step, year by year. It was not that he was a bigger boy among the big boys. He was a newer man among those in whom Christ is formed and working.

It was not as though Cliff Johnson had no meaningful spiritual depth during his first seventy-seven years of life. Christ's baptismal grace was alive and real in him from his earliest days, nurtured by a family whose spiritual fiber was tested aplenty by drought, dust, the Depression and then the death of a brother in his teens. His meteoric career in radio and the fast lane life with celebrities did present danger zones laden with land mines for the soul. Luella was his spiritual anchor through it all, but when she was diagnosed with pancreatic cancer that role was reversed. Now it was Cliff who ministered to her. In carrying that out for over two years he had to receive inwardly before he could give outwardly. The daily caregiving, the Scripture readings, the prayers, the hymns, the times of talking and the silent spaces of just being there for each other were all part of the mystery of how human weakness becomes the crucible in which the Divine strength is given. A phrase for it comes from the doctrinal writings of the Lutheran tradition: "the mutual conversation and consolation of believers." It is viewed as a kind of third sacrament after baptism and communion. The rallying of souls under duress that comes from speaking the truth in love. Those hard days of watching Luella weaken and then suffer intensely toward the end were terrible for them both. Yet it was in this very experience that a rivulet of the Spirit kept flowing beneath the wintry bleakness of creeping death. Sunday worship became an oasis not to be missed. The support of family and the community of faith touched him deeply. After Luella's death, Cliff participated in the life of the congregation as never before. His distinctly resonant voice was heard in the church as Cliff became one of the lectors in Sunday and holiday services. He put his administrative and persuasive skills to work as a member of the Stewardship Committee and brought a positive energy to the meetings which always need that lift. When Grace's pastor, Bruce Modahl, invited him to become an assisting minister at the altar, writing and speaking the prayers and assisting in the liturgy, it had a meaning more profound than most had any way of knowing. Nearly six decades earlier he had delivered short homilies on the Lutheran Vespers program in Sioux Falls that was part of his pre-ministerial training at Augustana College. Leading in prayer and worship at the Grace Church altar closed a circle that had long been incomplete. He spoke of it often with Luella and she would sometimes respond with her own visions of how she might have been the pastor's wife, pouring tea at church gatherings or welcoming guests at the parsonage door.

Cliff's daily care and keeping of Luella throughout her two years of battling cancer deepened his life in Christ with a renewed awareness of what it meant to live—as the church fathers of old put it—*sub specie aeternitatis*—under the hope of eternity. Not too long after Luella's death in

1993 he had to apply that conviction to his own dilemma of prostate cancer. It began with a routine blood test in November, 1994. Dr. John Walsh, his family physician, had been red flagging the rising PSA count during regular checkups. A biopsy at West Suburban Hospital brought the bad news. Three doctors came in and stood at the foot of his bed and Cliff knew that it didn't take three men in white coats to bring good news. One doctor began: "Mr. Johnson, I listened to you on the radio for many years while I was growing up," a well-intentioned line that brought somewhat forced smiles to the faces of the other two. Then the second laid it on the line: "Mr Johnson, you have a testicular tumor in your prostate." Cliff greeted the news by pulling the sheets up over his head, engulfed in fright. He was hurt and angry as he murmured "why me?" A long silence followed, broken finally by his question about his chances. The surgeon replied that he couldn't answer until surgery took place and the options were known. Cliff asked what the options were. He was told that shots each month, chemotherapy, radiation, or surgery were all possible options. For a man of eighty, the doctor went on, shots, chemo, and radiation were not good choices. What then? Cliff asked. The answer was surgery to remove the testicular tumor. At that, everything that had to do with maleness in Cliff Johnson's body reacted with a strong "No!" But he had to face the inevitable and asked when the surgery would take place. It would be the following morning. With that the conversation ended. A note of comforting humor came later that day, however, when an African American nurse with long experience in these matters told him that lots of men go through the surgery and beat the cancer. She gave him a homey metaphor in which to place the next day's procedure: "Mista Johnson, it's just like crackin' eggs." Cliff's own sense of humor kicked it and with that phrase in mind he decided that it was better to hope than to despair. The tumor was removed successfully. Metastasis did not follow. He was cancer free. He was also more mindful of living with hope for the present as well as for the eternal. A wise, experienced, humane black nurse had mixed humor with professional knowledge as she became a messenger of providence. He knew that his body was not the same but the price was well worth it. His soul was intact and stronger than ever.

CHAPTER 8

A Calling Finally Clarified

The deeper, broader reach of Cliff's life of faith ran parallel with another renewing experience in the 1990's, this one centered in his mind. It came in the form of a decision at age 75 to return to the college classroom to complete his bachelor of arts degree after a hiatus of more than a half century. That two-year effort led to further study at the graduate level. He went on to earn a Master in Religion degree at the quite mature age of 86.

What launched him into this dusting off of academic skills so long on the shelf (he had not been in a classroom since 1936) was a serendipitous moment on an autumn day in 1990 when he stood gazing out his front window toward the buildings of Concordia University across the street. He turned to Luella and told her of the question running through his mind: why not finish the college degree? There was Concordia right in front of him. He had time now that he didn't have before. Certainly the desire was not lacking; he had never entirely laid aside the idea of doing away with the dropout baggage. But he wasn't sure whether Concordia would regard him as degree material. Luella heard him out and responded with her customary formula—cautious endorsement. Using her favorite term for her husband, she reminded him—"Dad, you're 75 you know." But she said it with a smile and tone of voice that signaled she was for him. She also knew from a half century of married life that what he set his mind to do would be done. It was worth a try.

He took the plunge and made an appointment to inquire into the prospect. His initial contact at Concordia could not have been more fortuitous. Dr. Elaine Sipe, new to Concordia from Belmont Abbey College in North Carolina, was in the process of setting up a degree program in organizational management. Cliff walked into her office, introduced himself, and got right to the point: "I want to finish a degree I started at a Lutheran college in South Dakota over fifty years ago." She paused, gave him a long look, arose from her side of the desk and took a chair beside him to hear more of his story. He told her of his two years at Augustana, the pre-ministerial curriculum, and the financial circumstances that required his leaving school. An important moment followed. Cliff Johnson was her first student in a program not yet fully in place. She could have put him off for that reason, and understandably so. More than that, of course, she could have implied that student applicants in their 75th year would be better off trying other schools more experienced in geriatric admissions. But she met him where he was, then and there, and did nothing to dampen his desire to complete a longstanding, nagging ambition. To the contrary, she outlined the requirements for the degree, encouraged him to contact Augustana College promptly for the transcript of his records there, and sent him home with a sheaf of application forms. Any questions she might have had about his seriousness were set aside when he returned with them filled out, in full, within days. He took further entrance examinations to qualify for enrollment and came through impressively. Dr. Sipe was his principal mentor for the classwork that was underway in the winter of l991. He signed on for twelve credit hours a semester and finished his degree within eighteen months.

Sipe kept a mentoring eye on his classroom work via contact with his professors and was gratified to learn that he related well to fellow students young enough to be his grandchildren, sought no favors because of his age and experience and refrained from excessive classroom reference to his experiences with celebrities, business executives and world leaders of international fame. Above all, he delivered the goods academically as his grades showed. He did have to miss a Monday night class early on, however, and explained that as president of a national travel association he had to be out of the country on that day. It was an excused absence without precedent and the only class he had to miss.

Despite his effort to make no waves as a student, his radio and community reputation were well known, especially in the faculty. That proved beneficial in surprising ways. One evening as Cliff was shopping at a local supermarket he met Prof. William Lehmann in the store. Lehmann knew Johnson both as a Concordia student as well as a fellow parishioner at Grace Lutheran Church. The conversation turned to the subject of the Senior Project Paper, a requirement for the B.A. degree. Lehmann was advisor to the Environmental Awareness Club on campus and suggested that Cliff might consider a topic in the environmental field. What began as an impromptu conversation at the fruit and vegetable department of the local supermarket turned into a Senior Project Paper and then some. The topic was Recycling At Concordia. Until this time there was no environmental conservation program on campus. In the course of developing his paper, Cliff contacted Concordia President Eugene Krentz and the Vice-President for Administration, Dr. Fred Spurgat, the Student Association President, Curtis Smith, as well as George Strom, president of the Roy Strom Company, the local firm contracted to do the pickup and handling of recycling materials from the campus. The result over time was the first recycling program in which the Concordia community was fully engaged. The longer term consequence of Cliff's Senior Project did not end with Concordia. He expanded its scope to the village of River Forest by contacting the Director of Public Works, Gregory Kramer, for discussion of a wider application of what he had done at Concordia. A cooperative expansion of the recycling program in River Forest resulted, as well as a new linkage between Concordia and the municipal leadership of the town—something much needed and a sign of a role in campus and community relations that Johnson would take on with increasing effectiveness throughout the decade of the 1990's. The

Senior Project paper had covered a wide swath of practical usefulness, an indicator not only of the quality of academic work that the 75-year-old student was capable of. It was also a hint of the beneficial connection between Cliff, the student, and Cliff the advocate for Concordia, in new and broader relationships to the surrounding communities.

The origins of that role began before Cliff became a student at the University. In 1986 Cliff had his first contact with the Concordia President, Dr. Eugene Krentz. The occasion was the launching of a community volunteer service that came to be called the Volunteer Center of Oak Park. Cliff teamed up with an activist local pastor, Rev. Don McCord of Austin Boulevard Christian Church, on a program at United Lutheran Church in Oak Park devoted to ways of giving back to the community. The lively response to the subject of volunteering included one woman's offhand suggestion—one of those throwaway comments easily forgotten—"We ought to get organized, shouldn't we?" But it stuck in Cliff's mind and simmered there until it moved him to do something. As president of the Lion's Club he passed the idea on to John Clark, the Club secretary and indefatigable volunteer for numerous worthy community causes, who agreed that indeed something should be organized. Cliff then sought out the advice and cooperation of another key Oak Park person, Virginia Cassin, who lent her support and prestige as a pillar of the community. Cliff put up one half of the initial $4000 needed to get the Volunteer Center off the ground and persuaded the Lion's Club to come up with the other half. The local Community Chest Agency offered the initial office space. The press gave the idea good coverage. The stage was set for launching the venture at a community luncheon, planned by Cliff with John Clark, and featuring the widely known University of Chicago theologian, Martin Marty, as the keynote speaker. Marty had been a two year resident of Oak Park in the early 1950's as a young assistant pastor at Grace Lutheran Church and thus knew personally of the can-do spirit that made Oak Park ripe for a more organized approach to volunteerism.

Among those present in the kickoff luncheon was Dr. Eugene Krentz of Concordia. The year was 1985, a date worth noting for the significance of the conversation Krentz had with Marty following his speech. They had been on opposite sides in a bruising denominational conflict that had been convulsing the Lutheran Church—Missouri Synod, including Concordia as an institution of the Synod, for ten years. That fact notwithstanding, Krentz heard Marty with appreciation for the subject at hand that had nothing to do with church fights. Krentz, together with one of his Concordia colleagues, Robert Prelogar, sought Cliff out after the meeting for a brief conversation. The two did not know each other well but were aware of the potential for the public good in the proposed Volunteer Center idea (which, incidentally, grew in 12 years to a staff of six with a budget of $170,000, engaging some 700 community volunteers annually in a wide variety of community services). Cliff tucked away in his memory Krentz's suggestion to talk further sometime. That happened two years later when once again it was Prelogar who arranged a Krentz-Johnson conversation. The Concordia president was increasingly conscious of the need for the school to outgrow its reputation of isolation from much of the life of the community. It was generally respected, but distant from most townsfolk whose principal contact with Concordia was through its students who were trustworthy babysitters, good hires for lawn care and dependable helpers with housework. Krentz sought to make the University's broadening liberal arts curriculum more attractive to any prospective students, not limiting its academic program to its traditional role of preparing young Lutherans to teach in Lutheran schools throughout the nation. He saw in Cliff Johnson the ideal person to help it happen.

The two sat down for lunch in June, 1989, again with Prelogar setting up the meeting and present as a participant in the conversation. Before the dessert was served Krentz had suggested to Johnson that he should be an applicant for membership on the Board of the Concordia Foundation. It took him by surprise. In gathering his thoughts before committing him self to an answer, he posed a question that touched upon a potential sore spot: "Dr. Krentz, you know where I go to church, do you not?" Krentz indeed knew that Cliff was a long standing member of the congregation located on a corner of the Concordia campus. His answer was as direct as Cliff's question: "We can live with that…" It was a courageous move on Krentz's part. It was also a prudent one, since Cliff Johnson was second to none as the best person to help Concordia reach out into the community. Cliff asked for time to think it over during which he conferred with Pastor Dean Lueking of Grace Lutheran Church. His response was simple and quick: "Go for it, Cliff!"

A brief sketch of the context of the Krentz invitation and Cliff's response is useful. Grace Church and its pastor had been on the other side of Concordia and the Lutheran Church—Missouri Synod during the twenty year conflict that raged through the denomination during the 1970's and 80's. Grace had been the parish home of the majority of Concordia faculty from the 1920's onward. For decades it's parochial school had been the laboratory school for Concordia's student teachers to do their practice teaching. In 1970, when the first tremors of denominational upheaval were felt, Grace Lutheran Church counted some sixty Concordia faculty in its parish membership. By 1990 that number had shriveled to a half dozen, a commentary on the local impact of the denomination-wide ruckus. The rift between the congregation and the University had also widened from 1977 through 1985 during an eight-year legal battle as the Missouri Synod contended for the Grace building and property. The divisive struggle drew national attention and went all the way to the United States Supreme Court before final settlement in the congregation's favor. Thus the once close and cordial ties between Grace and Concordia had been severely strained throughout the 1970's and '80's. Against that background, President Krentz's outreach to Cliff Johnson was notable. It was the first sign in over fifteen years of any outreach from Concordia toward a Grace parishioner for participation in a University program. Both Johnson and Lueking welcomed it as an omen of better things to come.

At his first meeting with the Foundation Board of fifteen loyal Missouri Synod men and women seated around the circle, Johnson was asked to introduce himself with a few sentences. He did not exclude his Grace Church affiliation (well enough known already) before going on to emphasize his desire to serve the University well through his breadth of experience in the community. From that initial meeting onward into the coming years he experienced no animosity or distancing because of his parish affiliation. As Cliff put it, he "put no dog in the fight." It was not in him to look for needless conflict. And he knew that even if he would have tried he could never have kept a foot in both camps with benefit to both.

After Cliff became a student at Concordia early in 1991, his subsequent recycling program was an early form of subsequent ventures he initiated to put Concordia more before the public eye. His Foundation Board participation from 1992 onward meant increasing contact with the University faculty and administrative leaders who urged him to continue the pursuit, of every way possible, to move the institution into the community. With that mandate as motivation, he turned his attention to the campus sound studio that had been organized by Rick Richter, director of the University communications staff. The basics for a television studio were there but no campus telecast program had yet been developed. In fact no cable based program had emerged anywhere in the surrounding communities for outreach to a viewing audience of several hundred thousand potential. By 1992, when Cliff had completed all the requirements for his bachelor's degree, he had made significant contacts with area clergy and other community leaders in connection with his Master's thesis study in the religious heritage of Oak Park and River Forest. That gave him a natural lead for a television program from the campus that would recall the community's religious heritage and interpret it to the present time. He named the program "The Community," intending that it be just that, a Concordia-based program not inwardly focused but aimed outward toward the community. He made the necessary arrangements with a local cable station. He put to use the format best known to him throughout his decades on the air, interviewing people with an art for getting at who they really are as persons, then teasing out their stories, experiences and how they saw religion at work in the present. He wrote and produced the program himself. And he did it all gratis for two reasons. There was no University budget for it, and he could do the program his own way. There was a payback to him, however, that was beyond any paycheck. In 1994 Cliff was in the early stages of the hardest transition of his life as a widower new to the no-man's land of grief and loneliness following Luella's death. Throwing himself fully into something for which his talents were an ideal fit helped fill the emptiness of a life without Luella and give him at least an initial answer to the haunting question of what he, as a man already in his late 70's, was still good for.

His trial run featured a program on a hot community issue, the controversial dismantling of the once prominent Wieboldt's Department Store at a prime location in the business community. Cliff and his Concordia video crew filmed the demolition of the landmark art deco building, a decision that had been opposed by residents who decried the loss of buildings with historical value. Proponents saw the razing of Wieboldt's as inevitable; the demolition was a visual sign of the transition to shopping centers made necessary by huge shopping malls that were rapidly drawing shoppers to suburbs farther out. Local business leaders Frank Paris, Village President of River Forest and James Hague, were interviewed for their take on the promise of the new direction and their voices carried weight in the community. "The Community" was off to a promising start, connecting Concordia with the community in a manner altogether unprecedented. President Eugene Krentz among those who viewed the series premier and sent a one word commendation— "impressive!"

Professor William Ewald of the Concordia faculty, a supporter of the series idea from the outset, was another early guest whom Cliff sought out for stories of how he and his wife, Carol, led groups of local elementary school children for summer visits to host families in Germany for a broadened outlook and sharpened language skills. Cliff invited to the Concordia studio the Dominican nun and president of nearby Dominican University, then called Rosary College, Candida Lund, as another guest in the series. Sister Candida's dynamic spirit resonated throughout the half hour as she spoke of her role as a nun, an academician and a college president who brought to the community notable speakers from near and far. Among them was Menachim Begin, the former Israeli Prime Minister. She recalled an unusual moment following Begin's impassioned speech. The subject was stirring, so was the speech, so was Mr. Begin's blood pressure. Having finished his address, he sat down to a dinner following. During dessert he had to take strong medication to counteract his still-high blood pressure. The medicine kicked in, causing a drowsiness he couldn't fight off. He dozed off briefly, seated close to Sister Candida. The audience couldn't miss the sight of what was happening. Non-plussed, Lund reached for the portable microphone and informed the audience: "Not only is this the first time we have had the Prime Minister of Israel as our honored guest. It's also the first time a Prime Minister of Israel has gone to sleep on a nun's shoulder." She smiled when recalling the roar of laughter her line evoked, including the bemused giggle of an awakened Menachim Begin. Lund's intelligence, commitment and humor were captured by the Johnson art of interviewing, and Concordia was well served by enabling a Lutheran campus-based program to air a winsome view of the Catholic educator down the street.

Among the scores of other program guests were Martin Noll who spoke of what it took to begin a community bank from scratch, one that intentionally remained independent of entangling mergers in its dedication to the immediate community and what it took to keep it that way. Don Offermann, the superintendent of the Oak Park-River Forest High School told of his journey as a Lutheran pastor's son from downstate Illinois to his college preparation at Concordia and then his teaching and administrative leadership of the three thousand student institution, with all the satisfactions and headaches that go with it. His successor, Susan

Bridge, was another program participant who brought the high school story forward to the new times and new challenges of serving youth from homes, races and social circumstances that constantly change and grow ever more complex. Various programs featured recollections of Oak Park's famed son, Ernest Hemingway, by the Hemingway historian and local high school teacher, Morris Buske. Arthur Replogle personified the deep local tradition of commitment to the larger good of the community with his review of changes in the local business community and his role in founding the Oak Park Development Corporation.

Among all the programs he continues to arrange and produce, Cliff values none more than the two special hour long interviews with the Cardinal Archbishop of Chicago, Francis George, and Professor Martin Marty, the Fairfax M. Cone Distinguished Professor of the University of Chicago. While Cliff's adrenaline flow surged faster than usual as he steered his two distinguished guests into the heady subject of the role of religion in shaping society, he proceeded via the personal rather than the abstract. What were their roots? Who shaped their minds decisively at early stages of their lives? Marty told of his growing up days on the plains of Nebraska under the tutelage of his first and best teacher, his father, a Lutheran school teacher and organist who taught him to love God with his mind and instilled in him a lifelong passion for learning. Marty spoke of his academic specialty of studying the intersection of religion and society with illustrations from his own personal story which reflected the fundamental elements given him before he was well into his teens. Cardinal George spoke of his boyhood beginnings on the north side of Chicago and his early bout with polio. It left him with one leg shorter than the other and the permanent limp that went with it. He recalled the sting of watching while other kids ran and jumped freely. But he also learned the transforming power of compassion and persistence from those who cared for him. From those early experiences he formed lasting convictions about the constant need for religion to leaven society through those whose motivation lasts through thick and thin. Living with his own handicap gave him a hidden treasure in his ministry as a parish priest to those on the margins. It also gave him a confidence to limp without apology or embarrassment to the papal chair of John Paul II in St. Peter's to receive his red hat and cardinal's ring.

Week after week the half hour Friday evening telecast continues to air programs from the Concordia campus that speak to the community at large. Cliff keeps arranging, producing and hosting "The Community" with guests from across the community spectrum—notable leaders, single moms, young adults starting out and seniors with long memories. Letters and calls in response to the programs are often appreciative and sometimes critical. But they keep him and the Concordia leadership aware that this unique university-based television program continues its mission of linking Concordia with significant events well beyond its campus. For Cliff, discovering that octogenarians do indeed have much to offer is satisfaction enough and more gratifying than whatever pay his efforts might bring.

Several years after he completed his bachelor of arts degree at Concordia, a chance remark set him to thinking about going on to graduate study and a Masters Degree in Religion. Again it was his earlier mentor, Elaine Sipe, who was there at the right time with the right word. Meeting her in the hallway at Concordia one day he struck up a conversation on what she was doing. "I'm doing a Master's Degree program, Cliff—why don't you do the same?" His "OK" was quick and offhand. But the more he thought about it the more he thought favorably of doing it.

Several years prior to the Sipe conversation he had done an independent project of developing a video narrative on a century of Judeo-Christian presence in the Oak Park and River Forest. He had come to it via his fascination with the interplay of Protestant and Catholic populations, beginning with his earliest experience with the best and worst of the subject during his growing up years. In the 1920's and following it was regularly an occasion for raised eyebrows when a Scandanavian Lutheran would even try to date an Irish Catholic. But not always. Cliff grew up with parents who were more ecumenical than most, within the limits of their time and place. The subject had also entered into his college religion courses and seminary aspirations and stayed with him. It was in 1998, then, when Cliff was heading into his 83rd year that he got busy. He selected twenty-five men and twenty five women from nearby Protestant, Catholic and Jewish congregations and began filming the interviews. The format was consistent. What were their stories, the experiences of their forbears, the fortunes of their congregations that stretched over the generations. What boundaries were crossed? Which were not? What honest differences were faced and what did their respective religious traditions say to them, if anything, in distinguishing between cultural and religious differences? Cliff knew from his own past, as well as from his research that that line is not easily drawn, especially in the theologically challenging relationship of Christians to Jews. For the most part, his interviewees cited cultural narrowness rather than genuine theological differences as the primary force at work in denominational relationships—or the lack of them.

The examples were numerous. Nancy Dillon reached back sixty years to recall her boldness as a Catholic (and a stellar tennis-player) in applying for membership in the River Forest Tennis Club. She broke the Club's long standing taboo against Catholic members and, when accepted, took great pleasure in writing in boldest, capitol letters ROMAN CATHOLIC on the litmus-test line regarding religious affiliation. Rabbi Victor Mirelman of River Forest told of the local versions of the old, sad story of the exclusion of Jews, especially in social relationships. As he put it, Jews were owners of stores, dentists and doctors who cared for the ailing and lawyers who handled legal affairs. But after 5 p.m. the curtains of separation came down and the Jews went back to their own people. He expanded the subject to the darker haunts of anti-Semitism over the centuries, with the Holocaust of World War II as the most monstrous threat to Jewish identity and continuity. Paul Reicher of St. Luke's Roman Catholic Church recounted the stories of Catholics finally loosening the Protestant choke-hold on Oak Park and River Forest hegemony, quoting his predecessor, Fr. John Fahey's witty summary: "we simply outbred them." He also spoke of the progress in ecumenical relationships after 1962 and Vatican II through "living room dialogues," pulpit exchanges and visits of Catholic and Lutheran school children to each others' congregations for Services of Prayer and Scripture. Rev. Edward Hiestand of River Forest Methodist told of the reigning Protestant ethos in the communities since their founding in the 1830's and later reflected in the dumping of illicit whiskey barrels during Prohibition (Oak Park and River Forest were dry by law until 1979) as well as the harrumphing about Frank Lloyd Wright's tying his white horse to the hitching post outside the mansion of socialite matron Elizabeth Cheney when he would drop by for what the local gossips reckoned was more than a social visit.

Other samplings further support the main point of the narrative. Oak Park and River Forest mirrored the religious loyalties that were intertwined with the cultural biases of the times. The churches were havens for the sorrowing and at the same time bastions for the xenophobic. Johnson's video narrative was given generous air time over the local cable channel and was well noted. More notably, "The Historical Era Perspective View of the Judeo-Christian Presence In A Community" received the National Telly Award as the best documentary film of 1998. Cliff was rightly proud. Concordia was equally glad for one more effective move into the community A major assist in the production of the series came from James Kosinsky for his stellar camera work; he later moved up to become the director of media productions at Concordia University and a continual help to Johnson. Cliff had long since valued the importance of first rate technical talent in radio and television production and recognized in Kosinsky the latest in the long line of capable people upon whom he could depend.

The narrative project had a further use. It became the basis for the Masters Degree thesis as an expansion of the Judeo-Christian local story. It was a three year task to complete the thirty-seven credit hours needed in theology and sociology covering the years from 1998-2001. His presence in the line of graduating students in May, 2002, commencement (he was just one week shy of his 87th birthday) was cause for celebration. He was the oldest student upon Concordia had ever conferred an earned Masters Degree. He earned it in the department of theology and thus had a connection back to his unfulfilled pre-ministerial studies sixty eight years earlier at Augustana College. His family, his fellow students and friends raised the roof with cheers in the Concordia gymnasium-auditorium when President George Heider handed him his diploma. After the handshakes, hugs and high fives of the graduation ceremony ended, Cliff joined with his own family and well-wishers who kept the celebration going on the campus grounds outside the gymnasium. Then he made his way alone to a quiet corner of the campus to think, remember and look across the street at the empty house and the front window where Luella had endorsed his quixotic journey toward completing his degree. His view was blurred by the tears that filled his eyes.

A longtime friendship with the Christopher family of River Forest and Grace Lutheran Church took on new meaning during the 1990's. Cliff had known Walter and Maxine Christopher for fifty years. The Johnsons and the Christophers sat in the same pew neighborhood under the north balcony on Sundays at Grace. Walter was an attorney who had contributed uncounted hours of pro bono legal work for Concordia. Then, sadly enough, he was dropped in the 1970's when the new administration at Concordia took over without so much as a thank you note for his years of service. Cliff felt the sting of that inexcusable brush off given Christopher but put it behind him. Now, twenty years later, Cliff kept up the family friendship which included Jay, the older son of Walter and Maxine and Jay's wife, Doris. She was the founder and driving force behind the success of "The Pampered Chef," a unique business selling quality kitchen tools. Always on the lookout for enterprising people to take an interest in Concordia, Cliff invited Jay and Doris to a Concordia Breakfast, a regular event for area business people that he and Ada Johnson had started some years earlier. Over time the cultivation process continued, with assistance from Pamela Mattox, Lisa Baermann, and Alan Zacharias of the Concordia Development staff. Jay Christopher was asked to join the Concordia Foundation Board which put him in closer contact with major needs of the University. That, in turn, led the Christophers to make their first major gift to Concordia to upgrade dormitory and office facilities sorely in need of it. The donors took special interest in the solid Concordia reputation in the field of early childhood education, but were appalled at the inadequacy of the facilities to house the program which drew widely from community families with young children. The fruition of those early contacts of which Cliff had been an initial part was the gift by Doris and Jay Christopher of sixteen million dollars to build and endow the Walter and Maxine Christopher Early Childhood Center in the autumn of 2002. It was an important and healing milestone in the long term consequences of Johnson's determination a dozen years earlier to "put no dog in the fight" in the Grace Church—Concordia relationship. He was glad to be among those present that bright October Saturday of the dedication. President George Heider and other Concordia leaders expressed to Doris and Jay Christopher the genuine gratitude of the entire University community. Cliff's friend Paul Harvey was the Keynote Speaker. The official denominational publicity featuring this largest gift ever to a Missouri Synod school had eliminated the detail of the Christopher affiliation with Grace Church. Jay saw to it that it got back in.

Another facet of the Christopher connection brought Cliff and the Christophers closer together. They had known each other from Concordia Breakfast gatherings. Cliff had learned that Doris was writing a book on the Pampered Chef business and its mission to build family life. Cliff called her to express his admiration for the sheer drama of how a homegrown business could rise to major business stature (by the turn of the century more than 50,000 kitchen consultants were at work in a client base of over twelve million, with annual sales exceeding 500 million dollars) and still keep true to its deeper mission of impacting American families—a subject dear to his heart from his "Breakfast With The Johnsons" years. She invited him to come to her office, shared with him an outline of her book, and sought his ideas. As they talked further Cliff caught a sense of the power of the life stories of these tens of thousands of women and men who made up the strong family spirit of the company. Recognizing the potential of where his mind was moving with ideas, Christopher invited Cliff to visit the national sales convention in 1997, joshing him with the billing that he should appear "as one of our stars."

He accepted without delay and relished the experience. Johnson spent several days at the convention site in nearby Rosemont. As he mixed in with the kitchen consultants he did what Doris asked him to do—turning him loose among the crowds of kitchen consultants, greeting, interviewing, collecting stories, catching the infectious Pampered Chef spirit and asking what it meant to work for the person who got it all going. Their answer to the latter came when their president and CEO strode out on the stage. Company heads who rule by threats and bare-knuckle power gain grudging respect. Company CEO's whose business savvy, as with Doris Christopher, is inseparable from her role as wife, mother and homemaker, is given a loyalty that can literally be a force field at company conventions. She came up the hard way, making the decisive moves and doing the grunt work to build the business from ground up, a woman with whom every other woman working with her can identify. The power of the moment prepared Johnson well for what he was there to do, interviewing hundreds of Pampered Chef kitchen consultants and asking them to send him their stories in written form after they returned home. It took him a year to sift through and select ten from the many he received. At the Chicago Navy Pier convention of the company in 1998 he returned to present these testimonies in four shows to the mostly women audiences totaling over 5000. When introducing him Christopher asked for hands to indicate how many knew him from radio or television and a forest of hands went up. On the stage behind her was an identical replica of the Christopher kitchen of 1980 where it all began. Above was a billboard size projection of another household scene, the 1950's Johnson breakfast table with the family gathered around the microphone ready for the morning broadcast.

It was an intentional touch, linking the Cliff Johnson program emphasis on the family at table with the identical Pampered Chef mission of giving people the tools to gather the family around the table. Before him in the first row sat the ten women whose letters Cliff had selected. As Cliff hunched down and put his full self and voice into the reading of excerpts from the ten letters, a spotlight picked up the person quoted and her image was projected above the stage for all to see as well as hear. Then each stood to receive the outpouring of applause that followed. The effect was genuinely moving and deservedly so. The women were not promoting a product or gaining points with the leadership. They were entrusting their life stories to each other, some of them tragic, others joy-filled, but all of them contributive to the familial spirit that is the Pampered Chef open secret and undeniable strength. Cliff came off that weekend on Cloud Nine and much reassured that the people-centered interactive style that had carried him with audiences since the 1940's was alive and well sixty years later. He was, to give Fr. Flanagan's phrase yet another new twist, up there with the big girls. No, not girls. Rather, he was a guest among women of purpose and dignity whose quality of character and proven business skills in the marketplace spoke for themselves.

And now what, as Cliff Johnson's ninth decade of life approaches?

Among the likely answers to that question, this one stands out. It is not to underestimate the amazing buoyancy that has marked his years, his capacity to reinvent himself through career stages, his taste for new ventures, his love for people, his sure hold on core beliefs and the values that have carried him throughout the kaleidoscopic trajectory of his life journey to date. Color his life green as one who keeps on growing, looking for what's next, open to what can be done to make things better, ready to try what hasn't yet been tried.

That buoyant quality flowing through his years has a foundation, given him from his earliest years on the South Dakota prairie. It is rooted in the stories of the manger in Bethlehem, the cross on Calvary, the open tomb and the good news of the Savior Christ whose love keeps life ever buoyant. His signoff line used so often in so many circumstances is "Keep the fire, keep the hope, keep the love!" It's what he himself keeps doing, making the best thing now about Cliff Johnson's life story the fact that it's still unfolding. And in the eternal view of things, the best is yet to come.

Afterword

his story isn't complete without a brief comment on what's happened to the five Johnson children following their years of broadcasts from around the family breakfast table. I have enjoyed sitting with them to hear their memories of getting up early every weekday morning, being on the air, and then dashing off to school with no excuses for tardy arrival.

They certainly gave much to the program. It is interesting to hear them speak of what they have taken from it into their adult years. Foremost, they report, is the continuance of the strong bonds of family love, through thick and thin, that keeps them close knit. Being at ease in front of audiences is another benefit they gained from the many appearances and travels that were part of their growing up. Their mother would be happy to hear them speak of having no sense that their childhood was taken away from them because of their unconventional circumstances;. they did not then nor do they now think of themselves as celebrities but were glad to be themselves as the family next door. Another gain they spoke of is a better awareness as adults of how hard their father worked to keep the creativity going for ten years in an industry notoriously short on continuity. Are they happy it all happened as it did? With one voice they say yes. Would they want to do it all over again? Again, in unison, once is enough.

Where have their paths taken them? Sandra is a successful realtor in Elmhurst, Illinois. Pamela is a high school principal in Tucson, Arizona. Linda is a travel industry consultant. Vicki is a construction development financial consultant. Cliff, Jr. is in real estate sales and property title closings with occasional rock band gigs on weekends. Together, Cliff and Luella's offspring have added fourteen grandchildren and fourteen great-grandchildren to the family line.

Cliff offers these brief dedicatory tributes to two people in particular who have been so dear to him all along. The first is to Luella, who, in his words "provided the unceasing deep love, prayerful guidance, support, sharing and caring during all the fifty-five years we had together." The second is a salute to his 93-year-old sister, Doris Johnson Thurk, "still teaching piano, pillar of the church, driving her car and long time member of the Fargo, North Dakota, Rotary Club."

Last but not least, Cliffie speaks a closing word in his own voice. How better to close a book centered very much about that voice and the man behind it?

> *It took a long time to candidly reveal some of my life's stories. Hanging out both my sometimes soiled laundry and wonderful experiences on the public wash line is not to make myself a role model for everyone. But I do have a special afterglow that comes from looking back and remembering. I'm grateful for it all. Now that my ninth decade is not so far ahead, let me put the past eight in perspective: it's not a very long time once you get here!*